TRANSITIONS

CAC Publishing

Center for Action and Contemplation

cac.org

"*Oneing*" is an old English word that was used by Lady Julian of Norwich (1342–1416) to describe the encounter between God and the soul. The Center for Action and Contemplation proudly borrows the word to express the divine unity that stands behind all of the divisions, dichotomies, and dualisms in the world. We pray and publish with Jesus' words, "that all may be one" (John 17:21).

EDITOR:
Vanessa Guerin

ASSOCIATE EDITOR:
Shirin McArthur

PUBLISHER:
The Center for Action and Contemplation

ADVISORY BOARD:
David Benner
James Danaher
Ilia Delio, OSF
Sheryl Fullerton
Stephen Gaertner, OPraem
Ruth Patterson

Design and Composition by Nelson Kane

Cover: *Six Studies of Pillows*, 1493, by Albrecht Dürer (1471–1528)
Metropolitan Museum of Art. Public Domain.

Oneing
An Alternative Orthodoxy

The biannual literary journal of the Center for Action and Contemplation.

Oneing is a limited-issue publication; therefore, some issues are no longer in print. To order available issues of *Oneing*, please visit https://store.cac.org/collections/oneing.

Oneing

VOLUME 11 NO. 1

EDITOR'S NOTE

All things transition.
—Felicia Murrell

T HE COVER IMAGE by Albrecht Dürer was intentionally chosen to show how something transitions in one form or another
while the essence of the object remains the same. Dürer's pen-
and-ink drawings show a single pillow changing only in configuration.
He was a master at translating the ordinary into the extraordinary
so that the viewer could have a full sensate experience of the work.
I believe you will discover this phenomenon in this issue of *Oneing*,
which was curated in part by CAC Dean of the Core Faculty Brian
McLaren, who graciously agreed to write the Introduction and recom-
mended several of the outstanding contributors.

As with Dürer's image, the articles in *Oneing*: "Transitions"
illustrate the same theme but are interpreted uniquely by each
contributor. Some address the experience through poetry, as in Felicia
Murrell's "Liminality and Certitude" and David Whyte's "Santiago."
Others have written poetically, as in Sophfronia Scott's wonderful
article on "The Color of Thought," where her hope "for humanity, for
all of us, [is] working toward embracing our unity—the unity we share
with each other and our creator. Working on ourselves may seem like
a small thing, like we are all mere drops in the ocean. But we are an
ocean."

Still other contributors have taken a much more pragmatic or
didactic approach to the theme. In "The Transition of Founders," Wes
Granberg-Michelson, a globally recognized ecumenical leader who
has served on the boards of numerous faith-based organizations,

writes about the challenge many founders face when the time comes for them to transition out of the organization they envisioned, created, and animated:

> Founders almost always possess remarkable gifts of vision, courage, inspiration, determination, ingenuity, and persuasion that allow organizations to emerge and thrive. But the transitions of founders can reveal serious vulnerabilities which often accompany their gifts. When this fact is not recognized and addressed, transitions can turn into disasters. But when navigated with honesty and shared trust, a founder's transition can open ways to a creative new chapter for the organization.

Granberg-Michelson goes on to offer four "lessons" that might be helpful for organizations as they support and guide their founders through such significant transitions.

A powerful example of the many and graceful transitions experienced by a leader is found in "Transitions and the Roles We Play" by the Right Rev. Eugene Taylor Sutton. In his compelling article, Sutton writes about how he transitioned between the different stages in his life—from actor to corporate executive to bishop.

Even though Bishop Sutton experienced many job transitions in his career, he recognized that the various stages were the same vocation, offering an opportunity to "proclaim good news." Now, as he prepares to retire from his current position, he writes:

> The important thing is to begin the journey. A grace-filled transition into a future that God sees for you will necessitate taking on some spiritual discipline that will allow you to be open to new possibilities. In this journey, you will not *think* your way into your next job or ministry; you will *pray* your way into it. This means taking on a contemplative spiritual discipline that will facilitate your being able to discern what that future could be.

Bishop Sutton reminds us that life transitions simply change the shape of our underlying vocation. This brings us back to the analogy of Albrecht Dürer's pillow studies, where the same pillow can take many forms, yet retain its essence.

These authors are representative of a larger body of inspired work that I believe you will want to return to again and again as you prayerfully navigate the many transitions in your own life.

Vanessa Guerin
Editor, *Oneing*

Brian D. McLaren is an author, speaker, activist, and public theologian. A former college English teacher and pastor, he is a passionate advocate for "a new kind of Christianity"—just, generous, and working with people of all faiths for the common good. Brian is Dean of the Center for Action and Contemplation's Living School and podcaster with *Learning How to See*. He is also an Auburn Senior Fellow and a co-host of the Southern Lights conference. His newest books are *Faith After Doubt* and *Do I Stay Christian?* To learn more about Brian McLaren, visit http://brianmclaren.net/.

Felicia Murrell, a 2022 sendee of the Center for Action and Contemplation's Living School, is a certified master life coach and spiritual companion. As a former ordained pastor, she has over twenty years of church leadership experience and now serves the global community with a message of inclusion and integration. Felicia is a freelance copy editor and the author of *Truth Encounters*. The parents of four adult children, she and her husband Doug currently reside in Phoenix, Arizona. To read more from Felicia Murrell, visit https://www.instagram.com/hellofelicia_murrell/.

David Whyte is an internationally renowned poet, author, and speaker. His talks, which address everything from literature to leadership, heartbreak to healing, and mindfulness to mythology, weave poetry, story, and commentary into a moving, almost physical experience of the themes that run through every human life: joy and loss, vulnerability and vitality, courage and despair, beauty and necessary heartbreak. He draws from hundreds of memorized poems, his own and those of other beloved poets. David is the author of ten books of poetry, three books of prose on the transformative nature of work, a widely acclaimed book of essays, and an extensive audio collection. To learn more about David Whyte, visit https://davidwhyte.com/.

RICHARD ROHR, OFM is a Franciscan priest of the New Mexico Province and the Founder of the Center for Action and Contemplation (CAC) in Albuquerque, New Mexico. An internationally recognized author and spiritual leader, Fr. Richard teaches primarily on incarnational mysticism, nondual consciousness, and contemplation, with a particular emphasis on how these affect the social justice issues of our time. Along with many recorded conferences, he is the author of numerous books, including *The Universal Christ: How a Forgotten Reality Can Change Everything We See, Hope For, and Believe* and *The Wisdom Pattern: Order, Disorder, Reorder*. To learn more about Fr. Richard Rohr and the CAC, visit https://cac.org/richard-rohr/richard-rohr-ofm/.

THE REV. CAMERON TRIMBLE is a pastor and denominational leader in the United Church of Christ, an organizational consultant, an international speaker, a pilot, and the author of several books about faith and leadership. She is the CEO of Convergence, an ecumenical and interfaith congregational consulting organization. Cameron also serves on the Board of Directors of Stop the Traffik, an anti-human trafficking NGO, and Yes! Media, an independent publisher of solutions journalism. To learn more about Cameron Trimble, visit https://camerontrimble.com.

CATHLEEN FALSANI is a longtime religion journalist and author of several nonfiction books at the intersection of spirituality and culture, including *The God Factor* and *Sin Boldly: A Field Guide for Grace*. A member of the 2022 Cohort of the Living School, she lives in Southern California, where she runs Sinners & Saints Creative, a literary consultancy. To learn more about Cathleen Falsani, visit https://www.sinnersandsaintsconsulting.com/.

THE REV. WESLEY GRANBERG-MICHAELSON is a global ecumenical leader whose work has highlighted the intersection of faith with public life. He was legislative assistant to Senator Mark O. Hatfield and Director of Church and Society for the World Council of Churches, then served for seventeen years as General Secretary of the Reformed Church in America. Wes chairs the board of Sojourners, an advocacy ministry linking faith and social justice. He also serves on the boards of Church Innovations Institute and the Global Christian Forum. To learn more about Wes Granberg-Michaelson, visit https://www.wesgm.com/.

THE RT. REV. EUGENE TAYLOR SUTTON is bishop of the Episcopal Diocese of Maryland and senior pastor of the Chautauqua Institution. Formerly canon pastor of Washington National Cathedral and director of its Center for Prayer and Pilgrimage, he also served as a college chaplain, parish priest, and professor of homiletics and liturgy at Vanderbilt University Divinity School. Bishop Sutton co-founded Contemplative Outreach of Maryland and Washington, DC and is a contributor to the books *The Diversity of Centering Prayer* and *Reclaiming the Gospel of Peace: Challenging the Epidemic of Gun Violence.* He writes and speaks frequently on issues of spirituality, justice, reparations, and racial reconciliation. To learn more about Bishop Eugene Taylor Sutton, visit https://episcopalmaryland.org/bishop/.

Sheryl Fullerton spent her career in publishing as an editor, editorial collaborator, and literary agent. She has worked across a broad variety of disciplines but most enjoyed her work with authors in religion and spirituality, including Richard Rohr, Parker J. Palmer, John Philip Newell, Brian McLaren, Sara Miles, Tony Campolo, Phyllis Tickle, Diana Butler Bass, and many others. After her retirement, she continued to work with and advise a few authors but now devotes herself to her own writing, including a lengthy history of her pioneer Mormon family, essays, and memoir.

James P. Danaher, PhD is Professor Emeritus of Philosophy, Alliance University, New York. He is the author of nine books and over seventy articles. His soon-to-be-published tenth book, *The Disciples' Gospel*, focuses on the transition from the dualistic, subject/object perspective the world has given us to the unitive consciousness that Jesus promises his disciples in John 14:20–24. This transition from the dualistic to the unitive perspective is essential if Jesus' words are to become our own.

Sophfronia Scott is director of Alma College's Master of Fine Arts (MFA) in Creative Writing, a low-residency graduate program based in Alma, Michigan. The recipient of a 2020 Artist Fellowship Grant from the Connecticut Office of the Arts, Sophfronia holds degrees from Harvard and Vermont College of Fine Arts. She is author of nonfiction books, including *The Seeker and the Monk: Everyday Conversations with Thomas Merton*, and three novels, including her latest, *Wild, Beautiful, and Free*. She lives in Sandy Hook, Connecticut, where she fights a losing battle against the weeds in her flower beds. To learn more about Sophfronia Scott, visit https://sophfronia.com/.

Paula D'Arcy is an acclaimed author, retreat leader, and speaker. She is the founder of Red Bird Foundation, which supports the growth and spiritual development of those in need throughout the world. The foundation is also dedicated to the healing and opening of the heart. A former psychotherapist who ministered to those facing issues of grief and loss, her work has taken place in prisons and jails as well as at retreats dedicated to spiritual growth, Women's Rites of Passage, and writing retreats. Her best-known books include *Gift of the Red Bird*, *Waking Up to This Day*, and *Winter of the Heart*. To learn more about Paula D'Arcy and Red Bird Foundation, visit http://www.redbirdfoundation.com/.

Paul Swanson is Lead Program Designer at the CAC. He is a jackleg Mennonite and a part of the Community of the Incarnation. Paul and his wife Laura have two feral, but beloved, children who know a thing or two about contemplation as the immediacy of life. Learn more about Paul's work kindling the examined life for contemplatives in the world at http://www.contemplify.com.

INTRODUCTION

I used to think that things were real, and change was something that happened to them over time. Now I think that change is real, and things are events that happen over time. Change is the constant and things come and go, appear and disappear, form and fade away.[1]

THAT'S HOW I recently described a transition that has happened in my thinking through the course of sixty-six years on this planet. I tried to illustrate this transition by drawing from a passion of mine, fly fishing.

There's something about standing in the flow of a stream. There's something about casting my fly just so, in hopes that it will drift naturally on the current, mending the line when necessary. There's something about watching a trout rise to the surface and gently sip the fly in. There's something about feeling its strength transmitted through the line and then netting it and admiring its shimmering beauty. There's something about releasing it and watching it return to the depths. There's something about the constant motion of casting, the constant shifting of currents and weather patterns, the constant movement of the trout themselves. I explained being drawn deep into contemplation as I observe

> a seam in the water, a place where fast-flowing water meets slower or still water. What is that seam? It certainly is not a set of atoms; every second, one set of atoms is replaced by new ones. If we suddenly froze the stream to stop the atoms from moving, to capture that seam as in a photograph, the seam would no longer exist. That's because the seam, we might say, isn't a fixed and static thing. It's a pattern of things, a relation

and flow of things. It is temporary, contingent, more of an event than a thing.[2]

When my eyes move upstream, I see a hump of water in front of a rock and recognize it as another pattern, flow, relation, event. Then I broaden my view, consider the stream itself, and see it anew: a flow from springs to creeks to bays to the ocean to clouds to rain, an event in a majestic, life-giving cycle. I imagine the stream bed over a hundred years, its meandering shape shifting in the valley floor, its s-curves undulating like a graceful trout.

I look at the rounded rocks beneath my feet: before the stream smoothed them, they were jagged boulders on a mountain, and before that, bedrock under the mountain, and before that, fluid magma deep beneath the earth, and before that, space dust drawn into orbit around the sun. What I see as a solid round rock is just one event in a long, long story.[3]

But my reflection doesn't stop with water and rock: "Then I look down to see my reflection in the water, and behold! I realize that I too am an event, a flow, a pattern of relationships!"[4] This thought process leads me to the conclusion I quoted at the beginning of this Introduction: a transition in my thinking from seeing things as fundamental to seeing change as fundamental and seeing things as events in endless transition, patterns in a stream, relationships in an eternal flow of relationships.

Fr. Richard Rohr often recounts a story from seminary, when a professor ended the last lecture of the semester by saying that Christian theology has in many ways been more influenced by the thought of Greek philosophers than by Jesus' thinking. A case in point is the Greek idea of absolute perfection, the idea that if something is transcendent, it is unchangeable, immovable, absolute, and incapable of transition.

Because we want to lift God to the highest level possible, many of us were taught to conceive of God in this Greek category of perfection. After all, what's the alternative—*imperfection*?

To see God as faithful and trustworthy, must we forever think within the Greek categories that we were taught from childhood?

I remember another kind of visionary moment that came upon me many years ago, not standing in a trout stream, but sitting at my desk, preparing a sermon when I was a pastor at a beautiful congregation in the Maryland suburbs of Washington, DC.[5] I had been preaching through the creation story of Genesis, and I realized that the universe described there didn't fit with the categories of Greek philosophy. The universe fashioned by the word and creative character of God was not immovable. It was not absolute and incapable of change. It was not immutable or static or, in the Greek sense, *perfect*.

And yet this is this universe that God called *good* and *very good*.

In the Hebrew poetry of Genesis 1, God's creation was, simply put, in process. It started simple and grew more complex. It started in chaos, and order took shape. It started without life, and life "sprang forth" and "multiplied." A sentence formed in my head that day, and since I saw it, I haven't been able to unsee it: "Hebrew good is better than Greek perfect."

In other words, Greek *perfect* is static, but Hebrew *good* is dynamic. Greek *perfect* is sterile and changeless, but Hebrew *good* is fertile and fruitful.

This Greek understanding of perfection, it seemed (and seems) to me, had a certain logic and beauty to it—but it also hid real dangers, as Christian history has demonstrated. A monarch could claim that monarchy was God's will, for example, and therefore, monarchy could never evolve into democracy. Similarly, patriarchy, white supremacy, religious supremacy, human domination of the environment, and other related concepts could be understood as absolute, God-ordained, perfect, unchangeable, and therefore unquestionable.

COULD THIS DEEP-SEATED understanding help explain why so many Christians today remain chained to the past, unable to imagine that change could be for the better, unable to accept that the present order, while superior to the past for some, is still deeply unjust for many and therefore deserves to be challenged and changed? Could *sin* be better understood as a refusal to accept needed change, a refusal to grow, a resistance to the arc of transition that bends toward justice?

Sometime soon, I hope you can take a walk outdoors or find a place to sit and observe the created world. Seasons change. Trees grow. Rivers flow. Rocks roll downstream and go from rough and sharp to smooth and round. You can look in the mirror and sense the same reality in your own face: new wrinkles, new wisdom.

Perhaps you can look at this world in transition and dare to echo God in Genesis: *behold, it is good . . . it is very good.* Perhaps you can see transition as an essential part of that goodness that is better than perfection.

—Brian D. McLaren

Liminality and certitude are always
at odds with one another.

Anxiety thrums through the body, unmooring–
Pause.
Relax your shoulders, unfurl your hands.
Try a deep cleansing breath.

Give yourself to the earth.
Let Mother gift herself to you.
Let your feet hit the soil,
remember the patterns of growth,
the cycles of life.

Things bury deep. Things grow in the dark.
Things rise again.
All things transition.

In the radiance of dark, there is process:
the unfolding of mystery,

things words cannot articulate,

a threshold to freedom the mind cannot comprehend.

But the body feels,

the heart knows:

This is liminality.

The threshold of transition,

from death to life, from evening to morn,

from gestation to giving birth.

The unknown is a part of it all.

—Felicia Murrell[1]

Pilgrim

By David Whyte

PILGRIM IS A word that accurately describes the average human being: someone on their way somewhere else, but someone never quite knowing whether the destination or the path stands first in importance; someone who, underneath it all, doesn't quite understand from whence their next bite of bread will come; someone dependent on help from absolute strangers and from those who travel with them. Most of all, a pilgrim is someone abroad in a world of impending revelation, where something is about to happen, including, most fearfully, and as part of their eventual arrival, their own disappearance.

The great measure of human maturation is the increasing understanding that we move through life in the blink of an eye; that we are not long with the privilege of having eyes to see, ears to hear, a voice with which to speak, and arms to put round a loved one; that we are simply passing through. We are creatures made real through contact, meeting, and then moving on; creatures who, strangely, never get to choose one above the other. Human life is contact, getting to know, and a moving beyond which is forever changing, from the transformations that enlarge and strengthen us to the ones that turn us from consuming to being consumed, from seeing to being semi-blind, from speaking in one voice to hearing in another.

The defining experience at the diamond-hard center of reality is eternal movement as beautiful and fearful invitation; a beckoning dynamic asking us to move from *this* to *that*. The courageous life is the life that is equal to this unceasing tidal and seasonal becoming: and strangely, beneath all, stillness being the only proper physical preparation for joining the breathing, autonomic exchange of existence. We are so much made of movement that we speak of the destination being both inside us and beyond us; we sense we are the journey along the way, the one who makes it and the one who has already arrived. We are still running round the house packing our bags, and we have already gone and come back, even in our preparations; we are alone in the journey, and we are just about to meet the people we have known for years.

But if we are all movement, exchange, and getting to know, where a refusal to move on makes us unreal, we are also journeymen and journeywomen, with an unstoppable need to bring our skills and experience, our voice and our presence to good use in the eternal now we visit along the way. We want to belong as we travel. We are creatures of movement, but we have something immutable in the flow: an elemental, essential nature that gives a person a name and a voice and a character as they flow on. We take our first bubbling source and our broad, subsequent confluences and grow in the conversation between them, all the way to our dissolution in the sea.

We give ourselves to that final destination as an ultimate initiation into vulnerability and arrival, not ever truly knowing what lies on the other side of the transition or if we will survive it in any recognizable form. Strangely, our arrival at that last transition along the way is

We are creatures of movement, but we have something immutable in the flow.

exactly where we have the opportunity to understand who made the journey and to appreciate the privilege of having existed as a particularity, an immutable person, a trajectory whole and of itself.

In that perspective, it might be that faith, reliability, responsibility, and being true to something unspeakable are possible even if we are travelers, and that we are made better, more faithful companions, and indeed *pilgrims* on the astonishing, never-to-be-repeated journey by combining the precious memory of the *then* with the astonishing, but taken-for-granted experience of the *now*, and both with the unbelievable, and hardly possible, *just about to happen.* •

"Pilgrim" is an edited excerpt from David Whyte, Consolations: The Solace, Nourishment and Underlying Meaning of Everyday Words *(Langley, WA: Many Rivers Press, 2015), 165–168. Used with permission: www. davidwhyte.com.*

The Hero's Journey

By Richard Rohr

Whom does the Grail serve?
—Parsifal's crucial question after completing the quest for the grail

THE JOURNEY TOWARD wisdom follows amazingly uniform patterns in universal mythologies. The hero might have a thousand paths to walk, but there seem to be classic and constant patterns beneath our meanderings. Barry Lopez (1945–2020) mirrored my own belief when he wrote that the truth is best found by looking for a discernible pattern.[1] It is *no* surprise that *the* essential mystery of faith for Christians is not a credal statement as much as a Christ-revealed, but also discernible, *pattern*. We call it the *paschal mystery*. It is not so much something we *believe* as something we learn to do.

The mythic and liturgical acclamation is lovely: *Christ has died, Christ is risen, and Christ will come again.* Life will be death, failure, and absurdity, which can lead to renewal, joy, and beauty. This pattern is *inevitable, universal, and transformative.* It is almost the story line of every good novel you have ever read. For Christians, Jesus is the cosmic and classic mythmaker who reveals and lives this pattern for us and tells us we can trust it. Of course, if we have eyes, the pattern is everywhere, but we just don't want to surrender to it. We need a model and guide.

It is rather common to speak of two births that are necessary to come to enlightenment. The first is natural and biological; we must be initiated into the second and choose it. There is no certainty that it will happen. Thus, great spiritual teachers invariably speak of the necessity of conversion, search, and surrender. Before we are "born again," we basically do not understand. We are innocent, cynical, or trapped in passing images. Eastern religions call it blindness, illusion, or aimless desire. The Christian West tends to call this once-born state "sin."

Sin is much more a state of consciousness (or unconsciousness) than it is individual immoral actions. Jesus came to take away the "sin" (singular) of the world (see John 1:29). Without the spiritual journey, we have the strange phenomenon of people who supposedly avoid "sins" but are still in the state of sin. They don't cuss, drink, or run around, but do so from a totally unenlightened consciousness of fear, disguised self-interest, social convention, or even hatred of others who do such things.

Let's look at some of the normal patterns of the classic spiritual journey.

Out of a formless, uninitiated life, there somehow comes *a call*. It probably takes the form of longing, loneliness, desire, the knowledge that there must be *more*, or a falling apart of the game that once sustained you. The hero is somehow directed beyond their private self on a search toward some transcendent or larger goal. This call can come from within or from without, but the would-be hero is enticed by Otherness, by Mystery, what some would call the Holy. This is the first invitation to rebirth. At this point, your yes can take many forms, but eventually there must be a clear trusting and a clear *yes*. Many are unfortunately hesitant at this stage. There is no one to tell them what this holy longing means, where it comes from, and where it is leading—and that it is God.

The journey continues often with *a protective figure.* Invariably, there is a friend, a "god parent," a biography, a saint, or a mythical image which aids, encourages, and gives strength and direction to the would-be hero. The journey never happens alone. There is always a wise elder, a guardian angel, a patron saint, a spirit guide, or a wise teacher who somehow sends you in one crucial direction and

Quite simply, there is no room for God within us as long as we are filled with our false selves.

warns of the dangers and obstacles that will be encountered along the way.

Somehow, that guide makes you aware, like Jack Palance in *City Slickers*, of the importance of "one thing." When you come to the "one thing important," as Jesus said to Martha (Luke 10:42), you move almost instantly from profane space to sacred space.[2] There are always many demons and dragons to be faced, but invariably there is one overriding teacher or guide, whether that be Jesus, Buddha, or Krishna. Without that protective figure, you lack both courage and focus.

Although the negative side has many faces and forms, the positive journey is usually presented as *clear, simple, and beautiful*—although still mysterious. Actually, you need to fall in love with your model and guide. You cannot usually have many gods before you, or your ego will remain the god who picks and chooses which god to obey today. This was why the biblical prophets were always trying to get the Jews to love only Yahweh and no other god. It is good psychology, if nothing else.

NEXT, THE *threshold experience* normally happens, when your own system of logic, meaning, success, and truth breaks down. As the Swiss psychologist Carl Jung (1875–1961) wrote, a true encounter with the numinous is *always* an annihilation for the ego. It's when Perseus confronts the serpented head of Medusa. It's when Jesus feels betrayed by Peter, Judas, the crowds, and finally his own Father. It's when the modern pilgrim faces their shadow head-on, through failure, imprisonment, or accusation. For the adult to be born, the child must die.

The difficulty with an affluent culture like our own is that infantile grandiosity can be maintained well into later life by money, meddling, or moving away. Quite simply, there is no room for God within us as long as we are filled with our false selves.[3] As Jesus said, "Unless the grain of wheat dies, it remains just a grain of wheat" (see John 12:24). That phrase, by the way, is a classic initiation phrase used in the mystery religions of Asia Minor.

As the cocoon of the false self ("sin") is gradually let go, the true self stands revealed. The true self knows who it is, what it must do, and, most excitingly, has the energy to do it—no matter what the price. This is *the task* itself, the sense of vocation, the goal, purpose, and challenge that guides every hero's life. Quite simply, a hero is one who gives their life to something bigger than themselves. They are not just along for the ride. But that *something* must be larger than their own life.

We have grown *very* cynical about the possibility of true heroes. Feathering your own nest has become so acceptable that we largely substitute celebrities for heroes. Today, you are a "hero" if you make a million dollars and a fool if you give it away. To turn around the classic hero's journey in favor of self-interest puts us at odds with almost all known literature, legend, and oral tradition. It certainly puts us at odds with Jesus, Buddha, Abraham, and the saints. When someone cannot do greatness in some real sense, their life has no universal significance or transcendent meaning. They are disconnected from the "love that moves the sun and the other stars," as Dante wrote.[4] In that sense, their life is a disaster, literally "disconnected from the stars."

But there is one more subtle, but crucial, step. If you read spiritual stories closely, you will see that there is always *a task within the task*, a struggle alongside the struggle. It is not enough to kill the dragon, save the maiden, or even die on the cross. *The real hero's task is to keep love, to find humor, to maintain freedom, to discover joy, and to expand vision in the process of killing dragons.* There is no room for pettiness, petulance, or self-pity, or one is not, by definition, a hero. The sour saint is no saint at all.

Our real demons are interior, quiet, and disguised.

Our real demons are interior, quiet, and disguised. They often show themselves as the "noonday devil," which is that pride, negativity, or self-absorption that reveals itself in midlife and spoils the seeming good fruit of early accomplishments. Without spiritual disciplines and regular repentance, far too many of us win many battles but finally lose the war. How utterly sad it has been in my work to meet retired, bitter bishops; sad but "successful" priests; and angry old widowers blaming the world for their loneliness. They had no Sancho Panza to accompany them, it seems, as they tilted at life's windmills. They did the task, but not the real task.

THE FINAL STAGES of "the monomyth of the hero," as Joseph Campbell (1904–1987) called it,[5] are the issues of *return*. The hero typically receives some kind of *gift* or bonus at the end of their quest. Don Quixote is forever searching for the "bread that is better than wheat." Prometheus receives fire, Solomon receives wisdom, and Jason receives the golden fleece. Often, the hero receives the eternal feminine in the person of a fair maiden or queen or princess. The holy marriage is completed when they become one and live happily ever after. The kingdom is now healthy and fertile because the masculine and the feminine have become one new reality.

But the important thing is that the gift is given over *for others*. The grail is not for power, prestige, or private possession. It is always for the sake of the community, for the common good. I wonder if we even understand this stage anymore. Far too often, our concern seems to be developing our retirement account, self-serving politics, and polishing our personal image. No civilization has ever survived unless the elders saw it as their duty to pass on gifts of Spirit to the young ones. Is it that we are selfish, or is it that we have never found the gift ourselves? I suspect it is largely the latter. I don't think most people are terribly selfish. They just don't *know*.

There are no loners among the great heroes. There are no self-made heroes who clean up the town and ride off into the sunset. It is always obvious in the stories that many characters, advisors, and circumstances have formed them by the end—usually in spite of themselves. What the pagan mythologies would have seen as fate or destiny, Christian stories would see as grace or Providence. In either case, the hero is formed and created by their times, their struggles, and, most of all, their enemies. They never create themselves. They are *created*, almost in spite of themselves. They have tragic flaws but learn to use them—or let God use them.

In the final paragraphs of the story, the hero invariably *returns home*, back to their community. They rejoin the folk with their transforming gift. Odysseus must return to Ithaca, the saints must help us here on earth, and Jesus says his disciples will meet him not in imperial Jerusalem, but on the humble roads of hometown Galilee. Finally, the hero is a hero precisely because they know how to go back home.

Enlightened consciousness, viewed externally, looks amazingly like simple consciousness. Second naïveté can be confused with first innocence by the uninitiated. The sayings of wise elders look harmless and irrelevant to those trapped in the complex middle. True wisdom looks amazingly like naïve, silly, and even dangerous simplicity—although we would never say so in polite company. The Sermon on the Mount has been deemed poetic nonsense by 95 percent of the Christian establishment for two thousand years—and that, in a word, is why true spiritual teachers like Jesus are always marginalized, dismissed, killed, or, worst of all, worshipped. Then we can admire them at a safe distance, like a pious icon, but cleverly ignore both their message and their actual journey.

There is no alternative, no other way to understand, than to go on the whole journey. •

This article is an adapted version of Chapter Seven, "Separation—Encounter— Return," in From Wild Man to Wise Man: Reflections on Male Spirituality *(Cincinnati: Franciscan Media, 2005). Used with permission.*

In Times of Turbulence, Fly Loose

By Cameron Trimble

"Loosen your grip on the yoke," my instructor said to me, looking out the window at the clouds growing more ominous by the minute. I was early in my aviation instrument certification training, and we had decided to make the journey from Atlanta, Georgia, down to a small airport near Panama City Beach, Florida.

I held the yoke of my aircraft between my pointer finger and thumb.

"Fly loose," he said.

"Roger that," I replied.

I looked out the window and couldn't see anything. I had no sense of the horizon, whether my wings were level, or our distance from the ground. I was in true "instrument conditions," relying on my flight deck panel to tell me that we were safe.

"We are going to hit some turbulence ahead," he went on, "and you will learn something about your airplane I hope you never forget."

I looked over at him. He continued, "These machines are made to fly. They are designed to maintain steady, stable flight. If you tighten your grip on the yoke, you reduce the aerodynamics of your aircraft. You, as the pilot, actually make the flight less safe, steady, and stable. So, remember: When the going gets rough, fly loose on the yoke."

The wind came at us suddenly, tossing us all over the place. Every instinct in me said to grip the yoke tightly to control the plane. But I kept only my fingers on the yoke, offering small corrections to ensure we maintained a wings-level attitude. Within ten minutes, we broke through the clouds, transitioning safely to the other side.

I've reflected a great deal on that lesson from many years ago. When you hit turbulence, fly loose.

Our world today is nothing if not swirling, turbulent wind tossing us around. In just the past few years, we have experienced economic meltdown, climate countdown, racial throwdown, political breakdown, technology showdown, and religious letdown. We are living through the breakdown and breaking open of much that has defined modern life.

In the face of such extraordinary transition, it's natural to look for solutions to our problems. In this way, we tightly grip the yoke of our families, businesses, government, and communities, trying to regain control of people and systems that feel broken and dangerous to our safety and survival. Of course, no amount of control will create the conditions needed to traverse these rough winds of change. In fact, authoritarian control may very well send us into a collective tailspin.

The great temptation in the face of disruption and destabilization is to locate the problem in a "broken system." Yet, "What if our systems are not broken?" my mentor and leadership consultant, Mel Toomey, once asked me. "What if something is missing?"

In the face of transitions, our first reaction is to move toward resolution. We engage in endless root-cause analysis. Yet, when something is missing from a system, there is no cause. We then must move in the opposite direction, looking for relationships that could generate the results we are seeking. These relationships have been present all along but have remained unlocated and un- or misidentified in the current

We are living through the breakdown and breaking open of much that has defined modern life.

system. When we move back and broaden our view, we grant ourselves access to see new possibilities in apparently random patterns.

When you fly 2,000 feet above the ground, you can see roads, neighborhoods, and even people walking around. You can't see changing terrain. But when you increase your altitude to 45,000 feet, you can now see that those roads, neighborhoods, and people are connected to a much larger landscape, one with mountains, rivers, and vast plains. Your altitude gives you access to certain views of the world. Changing altitude can broaden or narrow your understanding of all that exists in that world.

As Toomey once explained to me in a coaching session:

> What is missing today in our systems is a level of integrity that exceeds what has been needed up to this point in human development. I don't mean "integrity" in a moral sense, though it can have moral implications. I am speaking of integrity in a conceptual sense—integrity as wholeness. As systems evolve and begin to produce the results that they were designed for, they reach a point where they produce those results in such abundance that there is a breakdown. It's a breakdown in integrity. We as participants in these systems ignore "what is so" to a scale of dysfunction.

Certainly, we can see that the systems designed in the Euro-American imagination have reached the point of dysfunction. We have ignored the unjust impacts of that imagination which built its power on the transatlantic slave trade; the stealing of land, health, and wealth from indigenous people; the domination of capitalist consumerism at the expense of a sustainable planet . . . you get my point.

So, the world as we know it is transitioning from one grand imagination centering the supremacy of whiteness to a much larger imagination that holds greater integrity—wholeness—in a reality that has been present all along but unacknowledged to date.

This new world coming into being faces *genesis* questions that fundamentally shape our field of possibility. Will our political system serve the whole? Will our healthcare system prevent illness or promote it? Will we live in service to our environment or continue our path of certain destruction? Will our technology accelerate our learning and development, or will it generate new forms of control and oppression? In other words: Who shall we be in this new world, and what world shall we create in service of that being?

Professor and futurist Bayo Akomolafe pushes us to imagine even further. The transition we must undertake, he states, is one of a shift in *Anthropocene*, the understanding of humans as the center of the story. Akomolafe declares:

> Liberal humanist, modernist thinking situates humans at the center of the room: We are in charge, generally superior to all other kinds of life on the planet, and we live *on the planet*. . . . Quite literally, we are not the planet in its ongoing materiality—we are lords of the realm. So we think in terms of this linear, anorexic space. We live in this tiny humanist bubble, and we deal with the marks on the bubble, the hieroglyphics on the bubble.[1]

⚹

The greatest transition we must make in this point of human development is decentering ourselves as the most important characters in the story of cosmic creation.

⚹

Rabbi Rami Shapiro helps us understand this transition when he explains[2] how the Jewish tradition reads the creation story in Genesis 1–2. In this text, God creates light on the first day, looks at it, and says, "It is good." God's creation goes on this way, creating the sky, land, sun, moon, plants, and animals of the earth. At the end of each day, God looks at what God has created and says, "It is good." But on the sixth day, after creating humans and showing humanity all the abundance of the earth, the text states, "God saw everything that God had made, and indeed, it was *very* good" (Genesis

We must resist looking to the frameworks of the past to lead us into the future.

1:31). In other words, God looked at the sum of all of creation, everything living in balance together, and said, "This is *very* good."

It stands to reason that humans missed this essential lesson of interdependence. We now have the chance to learn that the goodness of all of creation is in its balance, diversity, and collaboration with the cosmic whole. This will require of us a transition in how we privilege ourselves within our environment: now honoring the living beings that accompany us, even in our blind denial of their equal value.

Making this transition in perspective will require new cultural stories. Philosopher and author Jean Houston often reminds us that our lives are "mything links," links between the great mythic stories, the great stories of all times and places, and the playing out of those stories in everyday life.[3] As "mything links" to past and present, we act out the values of these stories in ways that create the world we inhabit today. More importantly, we are also the "mything links" to imaginations of the future, for the stories we create and embrace today determine the future our children and grandchildren live tomorrow.

Our imaginal capacity has never been more important. We stand at the nexus of great transitions in our awareness: Climate change, nuclear proliferation, and the rise of authoritarianism represent real and present dangers to the survival of humanity and many other species on our planet. Humanity has a special role and responsibility in this time. Environmentalist Thomas Berry (1914–2009) stated, "Our challenge is to create a new language, even a new sense of what it is to be human. It is to transcend not only national limitations, but even our species' isolation, to enter into the larger community of living species. This brings about a completely new sense of reality and value."[4]

We must resist looking to the frameworks of the past to lead us into the future. Doing so is a way to pretend to control, to tighten our grip and reduce our cultural aerodynamic flexibility. Instead, perhaps we turn to ways of wisdom that cultivate intuition, patience, and ingenuity. We embrace the ways of a Mystic Wayfinder, one who purposefully gets lost in order to chart new ways forward. By getting lost and welcoming the reality that we do not have the answers or know the way forward, we enter a space of liminality and emergence. We are not attempting to fix "broken systems" but are, instead, summoning entirely new worlds. We open ourselves to experimentation and new discoveries of a world present all along but hidden by our biased cultural blindness.

At the end of many Psalms in the Bible, the psalmist concluded with the word "selah." While there is still some debate among scholars about its meaning, the general consensus is that it serves as a marker to the worshipper to pause, to wait, to take a breath. It's a moment of intermission, marking the ending of one movement and the beginning of the next.

We are in a "selah" time, where the urgency of our challenges invites us to pause, to wait, and to reflect more deeply. We must ask ourselves the questions of the Mystic Wayfinder:

1. Who are we?
2. How shall we be in holistic relationship with the creative cosmos?
3. How shall we work together to bring forth a shared vision for the planet and humanity?

WE DO NOT have the answers today. We have the wondering. We have the gifts of being lost to guide us. We must now use the wisdom of our wounds, both caused and carried, as portals into new ways of becoming.

In his work titled *Thoughts in Solitude*, Catholic monk and mystic Thomas Merton (1915–1968) wrote a prayer for such a time as this:

My Lord God, I have no idea where I am going.
I do not see the road ahead of me.
I cannot know for certain where it will end.
Nor do I really know myself, and the fact that I think
    that I am following your will
    does not mean that I am actually doing so.
But I believe that the desire to please you does in fact please you.
And I hope I have that desire in all that I am doing.

I hope that I will never do anything apart from that desire.
And I know that if I do this you will lead me by the right road
   though I may know nothing about it.
Therefore will I trust you always
   though I may seem to be lost and in the shadow of death.
I will not fear, for you are ever with me,
   and you will never leave me to face my perils alone.[5]

I think of this prayer often as the prophetic prayer for emergence times. His is the prayer for the disoriented explorer, the faithful pioneer. The comfort of his faith is in God's promise that even amid disorientation, he is not alone. God is with him, for him, and guiding him through the not-knowing. So it is with us all.

Bayo Akomolafe often begins his presentations with this call:

The times are urgent; let us slow down. Slowing down is losing our way. Losing our way is not a human capacity or human capability. It is the invitations that are now in the world at large, inviting us to listen deeply, to be keen and to be fresh and to be quick with our heels, to follow the sights and sounds and smells of the world.[6]

His is an invitation to become fully present to the unfolding wonder of the world around us, to let go of our need to control the narrative and be swept up in the possibility of a more just and generous future ahead. As an aviator and pastor, I hear in these words the invitation to fly loose on the yoke and enjoy the ride.   •

Standing in a Threshold

By Cathleen Falsani

T HERE ARE PRECIOUS few moments in life when we realize we are standing in a threshold—the betwixt and between, a profound liminal space—and have the clarity to know that when we pass through it, we will be forever changed.

I recall such a moment, sitting atop a king-sized bed with my laptop perched on a pillow in the house my family and I had rented in the Connecticut beach town where I'd grown up. It was 11:50 p.m. on the night before my mother's memorial service in October 2019, and I was staring at my not-quite-finished application for the Center for Action and Contemplation's Living School that was due at midnight.

I'd begun the process of applying much earlier in the year, when my eighty-five-year-old mother, Helen Falsani, was still alive. It was not long before I left my home in California for Boise, Idaho, where I lived with and cared fulltime for my mother. She had chosen palliative care and home hospice rather than waging chemical warfare against cancer when it returned for a third go at her in fifteen years.

When my mother passed from this life into the More on August 8, 2019, there was no green flash, no whoosh, neither earthquake nor palpable flapping Wild Goose wings. There was only inhale, exhale, and then stillness. Pneuma, Spirit enveloped by Spirit. She died peacefully in her own bed, just as she had wanted, holding my hand, just as I had hoped.

M Y MOTHER WAS a force of nature, a hurricane in high-heeled espadrilles with a matching purse. She was loving, adventurous, impatient, kind, long-suffering, maddening, magical, courageous, anxious (or "nervadood," as she'd say), silly, funny (intentionally and otherwise), warm, wondrous, faithful, and an Olympic-level spiritual bully. She was afraid for much of her life, especially in its last few decades, when she consumed a steady diet of fear and loathing via Fox News and associates. She was not afraid of dying, but of a growing list of living things.

Mom had been training for her heavenly departure, via death or the Rapture, for forty years, ever since she met Jesus as her "personal Lord and savior" at a Southern Baptist Bible study and abandoned her devout Catholicism, dragging her children and spouse away from the ancient liturgical rhythms of our ancestors into the big-top circus tent of American evangelicalism. She abided for many years on this side of the Veil with great anticipation for the moment she would pass through it to eternity, where, she believed, she literally would meet Jesus face-to-face. And I hope she did.

For those of us who remained in this realm, she left behind spiritual breadcrumbs—a few treasures and a lot of crap—as well as a legacy of pain, anger, and grief to navigate, each of us in our own way—which brought me to that Airbnb bedroom across the street from a beach in Connecticut where I'd spent countless happy hours playing on the strand as a child, staring at my laptop screen and the answers I'd crafted to the questions in the Living School application. I checked the time—only minutes to go—thought, "That will have to be enough," made the sign of the cross above the keyboard, and clicked send.

The next morning, we buried my mother's ashes next to my father's, according to her wishes, and held a service that included poetry from Mary Oliver, eulogies by both my brother and me, a bagpiper playing "Danny Boy" and "Amazing Grace," and 1,000 paper cranes folded by the congregation's children that just happened to be suspended from the ceiling above the wooden pews of one of the oldest churches in New England.

Three months later, I received word of my admittance into the Living School's 2022 cohort. I was elated and couldn't wait to begin my studies, marking new beginnings, spiritually and temporally. Then, six weeks after that, COVID-19 arrived, changing all our plans and the world as we knew it.

"What an awful time to open a new chapter in my ongoing spiritual education, studying the perennial wisdom traditions of contemplation and mysticism," I've thought more than a few times over the last two years.

Yes, the timing was awful—*and* it also was perfect.

That last bit is part of the hard-won wisdom I was able to cultivate during my tenure as a member at the Living School, which I've come to think of, in the very best of ways, as a kind of finishing school for middle-aged mystics (and those aspiring to be). Learning nondualistic thinking—in this case, that the timing could be awful and perfect simultaneously, not just either-or—is one of the foundational principles of contemplative spirituality.

A cradle Catholic exiled to the Wild West of evangelical Protestantism not long after I'd made my first Communion, I had spent fifteen of my twenty years of formal education in faith-based institutions, including private Christian prep school, an evangelical Christian college, and the United Methodist seminary where I earned a master's degree in theological studies.

Add to that the twenty or so years I spent as a journalist covering religion for mainstream media, during which I essentially went to

Learning nondualistic thinking...
is one of the foundational
principles of contemplative spirituality.

church for a living, and my religious education was robust long before I'd heard of Richard Rohr or his school. But as I approached my fiftieth birthday—entering what Rohr calls the "second half of life" as my mother was preparing to make her final exit—that religious education had begun to feel increasingly incomplete.

I yearned for something deeper that would widen the aperture through which I understand the Divine and the world, connecting my faith to a sustainable contemplative practice and with a wisdom tradition that is both ancient and dynamic. I also sought a new clarity of vocational and personal purpose. I wanted to be useful, a good steward of my gifts and experiences, in the "called and gifted for the Third Millennium"[1] sense of things.

It was around this time that two things happened: Someone pressed a copy of Fr. Richard Rohr's *Falling Upward: A Spirituality for the Two Halves of Life* into my hands, and then an editor at Religion News Service, for which I occasionally write, asked me to travel to Albuquerque in early 2019 to interview Rohr for a long profile in advance of the release of what he expected to be his final "big" book, *The Universal Christ: How a Forgotten Reality Can Change Everything We See, Hope For, and Believe.* Between *Falling Upward* and my conversation[2] with the Franciscan friar himself, where he blessed me with some wisdom for dealing with my mother as I moved back in with her for the first time in thirty years, I experienced an almost ineffable draw toward both the Living School and the Catholic spirituality of my childhood, something Rohr describes as feeling spiritually "homesick."

Rohr writes in *Falling Upward*:

> We are both sent and drawn by the same Force, which is precisely what Christians mean when they say the Cosmic Christ is both alpha and omega. There is an inherent and desirous dissatisfaction that both sends and draws us forward, and it comes from our original and radical union with God. What appears to be past and future is in fact the same home, the same call, and the same God.[3]

Rohr says our paths are never a straight line; they are spirals. Mine has certainly been that.

When my once-Catholic family of origin landed, of all places, among the Southern Baptists in southern Connecticut, we were warmly welcomed into their community, where I learned a lot about grace and ice cream socials. That led to a long sojourn in evangelicalism (during a kinder, gentler phase than the one it is experiencing presently), before I sauntered toward Canterbury and the Episcopal Church with its smells, bells, and liturgy in my early twenties.

Since then, I have, to borrow a phrase from an Irish friend, been "as comfortable and uncomfortable" inside a Catholic cathedral as in any other church, without any set spiritual home. Seemingly pilgrim-oriented since birth, with God-bothering ever central to my life, I remain a woman without a church—and I am fine with that . . . mostly.

Rohr even has a good word for my situation. "At last, one has lived long enough to see that 'everything belongs'—even the sad, absurd, and futile parts," he writes in *Falling Upward*. "In the second half of life, we can give our energy to making even the painful parts and the formally excluded parts belong to the now unified field."[4]

In the second half of my life, he assured me, all the seemingly disparate parts of my life and spiritual journey would fit and make sense. I had to transcend earlier experiences, unlearn a few things, but include everything: the Southern Baptist hymns, the mask of the Buddha I picked up in Nepal, and the rosary that was blessed by Pope Francis on the night of his election, when I stood among a scrum of other reporters in the rain taking notes and witnessing history. In my story, the Living School taught me, all of it belongs.

It also showed me that I could love my mother fully and despise her bullying, appreciate her great faith and reject its toxic theology. She was wonderful, and she was terrible. She was both.

THE LIVING SCHOOL has helped me (and more than a thousand other adult students since 2013) create "deep engagement with [our] truest selves and with the world."[5] Through contemplative practice and study of the mystic tradition inside Christianity and beyond it, the school invites students "to awaken to the pattern of reality—God's loving presence with and in all things."[6]

In the pre-COVID "before times," if you will, the Living School had a distance learning component. It is a school for grownups who are expected to be self-starters and invested enough in their education to read, study, and integrate the wisdom on their own without tests and quizzes or any kind of "proving." But there also were several large, in-person gatherings scheduled during each year of the program,

I was standing
in another threshold,
and I knew it.

where students connect face-to-face with our teachers and each other. The pandemic scuttled that for my cohort, the only one to spend its entire tenure beneath COVID-19's pall, when all events but our final gathering were relocated to Zoom.

At times, that made feeling connected to my classmates and our studies challenging. Even though our class of about 200 was broken into smaller "circle groups" of about ten people each, with whom we met regularly via Zoom to talk about what we were learning and our lives in general, and while we were grateful for the technology that allowed us to do so, it was a wan substitute for being together in person.

In late July 2022, when we finally were able to be together physically for a five-day symposium in Albuquerque that marked the end of our cohort's studies, all the pieces fit together in a way I'd never experienced. The wisdom imparted to us through the voices of St. John of the Cross, St. Thérèse of Lisieux, Thomas Merton, Julian of Norwich, the Desert Mothers and Fathers, Howard Thurman, Thich Nhat Hanh, and so many others finally put on flesh and walked among us, alongside core faculty members Richard Rohr, Brian McLaren, James Finley, Mirabai Starr, and Barbara Holmes (some of whom joined us via Zoom as COVID-19 health concerns persisted).

Hugging for the very first time many of the people I'd been praying and sharing an intimate spiritual journey with for two years was a precious gift: cool spring water after a drought that felt interminable.

When McLaren challenged us to not judge others, when Starr told us that grief is a spiritual practice, and when Finley urged us to ask ourselves, "All things considered, what is the most loving thing I can do right now?" we could see, hear, and feel their intentions and our own in the way humans are able to do only fully when they're in the same room. And when Rohr made his first entrance, arriving in a wheelchair with a health aide and his canine companion Opie by his side, he was a living, breathing master class of how to be fully present, not reactionary, and hold everything loosely—a lesson Mother Nature has been trying to teach the whole of humanity in the last couple of years.

Only a few times in my half-century of life have I been blessed with the awareness of something coming full circle, to see and understand the spiritual growth that has taken me from there to here. That week in Albuquerque was full of such numinous, transformational experiences—a turning point in a thin place.

I was standing in another threshold, and I knew it.

"God put us on this earth for a little space, to bear the beams of love," Rohr, paraphrasing the poet William Blake, told several hundred students assembled in the Hotel Albuquerque ballroom for the final event of the week: our "sending" as students who had completed our sojourn at the Living School.

"It's all an enduring, an allowing—allowing the beams of infinite love to come toward you, in every event, in every setting, in every relationship, and even in your own mishaps and faults and mistakes," he continued.

For Rohr, the Living School students, faculty, and CAC staff, the July ritual marked the end of a chapter and the beginning of something new in their lives too. There is a student group just behind mine, the 2023 cohort, but none after that. For now, the Living School admissions process has been put on hold[7] while the CAC leadership discerns what is to come next and how.

Also in October 2022, Rohr retired from his positions as dean of the CAC's core faculty and as a voting member of the Center's board of directors. He announced his intention to "step back" from public life.

"May you know the height and the length and the depth and the breadth, may you know the love that surpasses all knowledge," Rohr told us, lifting a hand from his cane to bless us with the sign of the cross. "And may you know that you are infinitely children of God."

I wish the same for dear Rohr, the Living School, and the entire CAC community as they walk together through this time of deep transition, into the sacred beauty and holy surprise of whatever comes next. ◆

The Transition of Founders

By Wesley Granberg-Michaelson

WE'RE IN A TIME when many founders are trying to finish well. The ferment of social movements and cultural change in the 1970s and beyond gave birth to many new organizations. They addressed world hunger, women's empowerment, racial justice, antinuclear efforts, peacemaking, environmental protection, combatting poverty, and much more, as well as spiritual renewal, youth ministries, intentional Christian community, liturgical renewal, interfaith relationships, and other grassroots initiatives.

Such movements were led by key individuals who could inspire and galvanize others around a vision of social, political, and religious change. As those movements took hold and tried to sustain themselves, they became organizations. The leaders who first catalyzed others around a vision became founders. Many served for years as their organizations grew and evolved. In the past decade or so, those founders have been facing transitions as they step away from their formative leadership roles.

Founder transitions, however, are difficult and fraught with peril. They also hold potential untapped promise. How and when these transitions occur can be decisive for the organization's future. Navigating these transitions with wisdom and discernment and including the shared engagement of the founder and the governing board—these usually arduous tasks can become more difficult and treacherous than originally anticipated. Such transitions serve as "stress tests," revealing the resilience or exposing the vulnerabilities of both the organization and the founder.

These types of transitions have been studied carefully in the private sector and among nonprofits. Such analysis often identifies that "founder's syndrome" complicates any process of transition. For example, one article, "How to Survive Nonprofit Founder's Syndrome," describes this as an illness requiring care:

> Nonprofit Founder's Syndrome is a common treatable disease. Frequently carried as a recessive gene by passionate, dedicated, dynamic, and visionary entrepreneurial leaders. Commonly found paired with groundbreaking new ideas to solve social problems. Often associated with new fledgling organizations.[1]

Founders almost always possess remarkable gifts of vision, courage, inspiration, determination, ingenuity, and persuasion that allow organizations to emerge and thrive. But the transitions of founders can reveal serious vulnerabilities which often accompany their gifts. When this fact is not recognized and addressed, transitions can turn into disasters. But when navigated with honesty and shared trust, a founder's transition can open ways to a creative new chapter for the organization.

While ample analysis has been focused on founders' transitions in private companies and nonprofits, far less attention has been devoted to these dynamics within religious settings such as congregations, denominational systems, and faith-based organizations. Considering the overlay of theological understandings, missional motivation, and various models of spirituality and leadership which are involved, navigating the complexities posed by the transition of founders in religiously rooted organizations is even more critical.

Through serving on the boards of several faith-based organizations as well as working with various congregations, I've had several opportunities to be engaged in the leadership transitions of their founders. Some have gone reasonably well, although always with challenges. Others have crashed in disastrous ways. Hopefully, I've learned some things along the way. Drawing from the wisdom of those with whom I worked, I offer four lessons that might help guide founders and those responsible for governing their transitions.

1. THE FOUNDER'S FUTURE MATTERS

WHEN I WAS involved in a particularly difficult transition, a fellow board member shared that we needed to give focused attention to what the founder would do in the future. "Most boards focus appropriately on finding the right successor," he said. "But if we don't accompany founders in helping them to discover a future where their gifts can continue to thrive, we may never find our way through without injurious conflict." In that case and many which followed, I've found deep wisdom in this advice.

Unless there are serious issues of health or age, most founders won't simply walk off the stage and go fishing. They are wired in such a way that prompts them to seek another challenge. It might be another place that welcomes their wisdom and gifts, or another book, or another innovative initiative, or some avenue which may not carry the same executive responsibility but will draw on the founder's unique wisdom and gifts. Boards often assume it's the sole task of the founder to figure that out. That's a mistake.

Founder transitions are most successful when the founder is being beckoned to a future that offers them a sense of excitement and challenge. It's the drive toward this new, inviting chapter, in whatever form, that helps the founder relinquish the control and ownership which they previously exercised, often for decades. Without this attention to the founder's future, a governing board risks a conflictive, awkward, and often damaging struggle simply trying to persuade or force a founder to leave their life's work.

2. THE FOUNDER'S PERSONAL INTEGRATION IS DECISIVE

THE PERSONALITY CHARACTERISTICS of a founder are key to their ability to lead a movement and create a thriving organization. These are relatively consistent among founders. We all know such leaders. With visionary courage, they set forth audacious, inspiring goals with certainty. That's what it takes to start something new.

But what are the potential vulnerabilities that often accompany the personalities of founders? In general, founders need and expect loyalty; criticism and critiques from others may be difficult to hear. Honest questioning can get interpreted as a lack of respect. Breaks in relationships may readily occur. Frequently, gifted associates are hired (chief of staff, executive director, associate pastor, etc.) with high expectations that they will bring managerial coherence to the organization, but they then depart in quiet, or sometimes public, frustration. Staff morale suffers.

These vulnerabilities become more severe if founders are locked into binary thinking—which occurs frequently. Things are clearly "right or wrong"; there's one correct approach, and all others are flawed. "People are either for you or against you." "We're on the side of clear moral and spiritual authority; others are compromised." So, for founders, it's often, "My way or the highway." Nuance is threatening.

Such weaknesses can become intensified in the founder's transition. Then, the degree of self-understanding and personal integration in the inner life of the founder become pivotal. If a founder has worked with their interior journey, whether through therapy, spiritual direction, journaling, peer group accountability, or other means, they are more likely to spot and manage personal vulnerabilities. But if a founder has spent years simply pushing ahead and not making self-examination an ongoing priority, disaster can strike.

This may take the form of a crisis of identity, where the founder's sense of self is fused to the organization that their gifts have built. The prospect of transition becomes deeply threatening as the end of their leadership is felt as deprivation, viewed with fear, and experienced as a loss of purpose. Often not openly admitted, this will seep out in ways that confuse and even derail the transition process. That's why it's crucial for founders to cultivate inner spiritual detachment from the fruit of their labor.

The challenges of founders in transition can be illustrated by using the Enneagram. Many founders are Enneagram Eight types. Of course, there are exceptions (Enneagram Three types are also often leaders, and other types occur), but it's helpful to focus on this example. Enneagram Eight personalities are strong, want to be in control, have a large personality, and are bold and assertive. They are comfortable with power and gravitate toward taking on challenges. When healthy and integrated, they learn also to develop qualities of being helpful, relational, and even tender. But the opposite can also occur—a sense that they know it all, don't really need others, and are invulnerable.

Chuck DeGroat has written a book of profound importance in understanding those patterns and pitfalls of leadership: *When Narcissism Comes to Church*. He examines each Enneagram Type and explores what happens when unhealthy narcissism infects the personality. For an Enneagram Eight, he writes this warning:

> While healthy leaders may display both strength and humility, the narcissistic challenger (Type 8) is invulnerable and potentially shameless. He lives his life to avoid weakness, and that requires him to protect any vulnerable or fragile part of himself within. He displays classic traits of a grandiose, overtly narcissistic personality disorder in his sense of superiority, his preoccupation with power and status, his expectation of others' compliance, his arrogant behavior and attitudes, and his interpersonal exploitation.[2]

At points of transition, the relative health or lack of integration in founders can burst to the surface. If such founders have worked

It's crucial for founders to cultivate inner spiritual detachment from the fruit of their labor.

sufficiently with their inner life, those dangers can be recognized rather than denied. Points of tension will certainly arise, but they can be managed in an atmosphere of relative trust and healthy mutuality.

3. THE FOUNDER NEEDS SUPPORT AND ACCOUNTABILITY

FOUNDERS ARE BRIMMING with self-confidence. Their certainty and trust about knowing the right thing to do, even when it goes against conventional wisdom and the sentiments of their group, enables them to break new ground. Such prophetic autonomy can function as a rare gift. But it also can create serious problems, particularly at the time of transition. Every founder must navigate the tension between faith in his or her own personal power to accomplish creative purposes and the need for patterns of leadership rooted more in collegiality and mutual trust. That balance, when understood wisely, needs to be continually recalibrated through an organization's stages of growth and development.

Some founders, usually those with less-examined lives, remain inflexible, trusting in their autonomous power and judgment to make the right things happen. Such founders firmly believe that they know best about both the timing and the process of transition out of leadership. They want to remain in full control. But in these cases, their individual discernment, inevitably clouded by an assertive, stubborn ego hiding deep insecurities, is almost always wrong.

Therefore, it is imperative for a founder to have a small circle of safe, trusted relationships to provide both support and honest accountability. In the transitions I've witnessed which have gone reasonably well, the founder has been accompanied in the process by a core group of such relationships. This is necessary regardless of the leader's relative health or evident vulnerabilities.

The prospect of making a transition out of the work of one's lifetime, even for healthy, well-integrated founders, brings grief, loss, and often pain. We make a grave mistake when we assume that the self-confidence and courage shown by founders in their leadership means they will know how to handle and navigate the emotional dynamics of their transition alone.

4. A FOUNDER TRANSITION CHANGES ORGANIZATIONAL CULTURE

Most founder transitions focus attention on the passing of leadership from one person to another. Often unrecognized, however, is the effect of a founder's transition on the organizational culture of the group. I've learned the wisdom of this phrase: "Culture eats strategy for lunch."

A founder shapes organizational culture, even without deliberately intending to, through their leadership style and simply the force of personality. The departure of a founder presents one of the best and most unique opportunities to alter and transform that organizational culture. Members and staff discover new opportunities to participate and exercise their responsibilities. Fresh open space is created. Expectations may shift. Power will evolve. Unrecognized gifts are discovered. New practices can emerge. But this doesn't happen automatically, and these changes can also spread anxiety in the organization. "The way things were done" with the founder provided security and predictability.

For this reason, the new organizational leader replacing the founder should give careful attention to tending and nurturing the group's culture, including how its governing board functions. It's a time to introduce and test new practices. This may include how meetings are structured, how time together is utilized, how personal faith journeys are shared, how biblical wisdom is engaged, how space for innovative ideas is provided, and/or how vision for the organization's future is fostered.

When a founder makes a transition, it's not only the leader that changes. Inevitably, organizational culture also becomes more fluid and open to change. Artful, discerning leadership can manage this process in ways that increase vitality and build capacity toward a

When a founder makes a transition, it's not only the leader that changes.

desired future which is no longer dependent on the unique gifts and commitment of the founder.

I N CONCLUSION, FOUNDER transitions are filled with promise and peril. Within the life of most faith-based organizations, such transitions are often managed more by anxiety than by wisdom. These four lessons, however, can help to minimize organizational dysfunction and build pathways toward the next chapter that continue to break new ground in the work of social, political, and spiritual transformation. •

Transitions and the Roles We Play

By Eugene Taylor Sutton

WHEN I WAS a student in college, I did a lot of theater. I wasn't a theater major, but I was cast in several productions, including playing Mercutio in *Romeo and Juliet*. To be sure, I did at one point consider a career in theater, except I was too wedded to the notion that I needed a guaranteed income.

One of the most important things I learned from my theater days was how to enter a stage. A good actor doesn't just appear or walk nonchalantly onto a stage and then start to embody his or her character. You have to be prepared to make an entrance, having already transitioned into being that character. The actor assumes the character *before* entering the stage. A lot of work has to be done beforehand to really get into your role.

Equally important is how you exit a stage. I'm reminded of William Shakespeare's famous line from *As You Like It*:

All the world's a stage, and all the men and women merely players; They have their exits and their entrances, and [each in their] time plays many parts.[1]

The bard goes on to write of our "acts being seven ages."

That wisdom causes me to wonder: If our life can be measured generally in seven acts or "stages," then what have been the stages of my life, and how did I transition between them? Also, looking to the future, how will I choose to transition to my next act?

I was a fairly quiet person as a young child, but my parents could testify to the fact that I was a different person as a teenager. They definitely noticed my transition from adolescence to my undergraduate years. My next transition was into playing the role of a corporate executive. While I was successful then, in terms of making a good income, I was not successful in living a good life. Having then heard the call to tend to my spiritual life and dedicate it to service, I went to seminary and was ordained into fulltime Christian ministry. Since then, I've been called to inhabit several roles, none of which I had planned to do and all which I am so fortunate to have played. So, when it comes to transitioning from one stage of development to another, or vocationally from one job to another, I can easily think of my life in seven or so "acts."

But here, I think we need to make a distinction between three related but nonidentical concepts: *vocation, ministry,* and *role.*

Your vocation is your life's calling. It's the consistent theme that runs through your life at every stage. Vocation, derived from the Latin *vocare* (which means "call"), is the call of the Spirit, that undercurrent in your life that's always flowing within. Frederick Buechner's description of vocation in *Wishful Thinking* is that "the place God calls you to

You don't get to decide what your vocation will be; you *live* into it.

is the place where your deep gladness and the world's deep hunger meet."[2]

Spiritually speaking, you don't get to decide what your vocation will be; you *live* into it. Perhaps Parker Palmer stated it best when he wrote, in *Let Your Life Speak*,

> Is the life I am living the same as the life that wants to live in me? Before you tell your life what you intend to do with it, listen for what it intends to do with you. Before you tell your life what truths and values you have decided to live up to, let your life tell you what truths you embody, what values you represent.[3]

So, what were you born to do? What were you meant to do? Frankly, I'm not sure that anybody really has a firm grip on what their vocation is until after age forty or so, when you find yourself saying, "So *that's* what all this has been about!"

I wasn't able to articulate what my vocation was until after I had already been ordained a Christian minister for about fifteen years. I put it in three words: "Proclaim gospel everywhere." Gospel is "good news," and sure enough, I'm always eager to speak the good news in whatever setting I find myself—almost to a fault. While I do recognize bad news—who can't, in these times?—I simply cannot live there. No matter how dire the situation, I immediately go into, "What's the good in this?" I do that because I'm *called* to do that; it's my vocation.

Being a member of the clergy is tailor-made for someone with my vocation. When I'm living into my calling, I'm in flow with the universe. But living into your vocation isn't dependent upon what job you have, or the setting or situation in which you may find yourself. It just springs up from the depths of your heart.

Your ministry, though, is different from your vocation. Ministry is servanthood; it is whatever you do to serve others, either as a volunteer or a paid professional. Someone can have several ministries in their career, all while living into their one vocation. In my own career, I've been privileged to serve as a college chaplain, parish pastor, diocesan staff member, cathedral canon, and now bishop of a major diocese in the Episcopal Church. In all these ministries, I believe I've been "proclaiming gospel everywhere." My vocation has been the thread that has transitioned me from one job to another.

But here's the rub. Over the years, I've found that many people pay far too much attention to getting the right job, but not nearly enough time tending to their vocation. When things are not going well or they start feeling that something's not quite right, they assume that the job or ministry they're in is the problem. "I must be in the wrong place," they'll say to themselves. Well, maybe the place isn't the problem, but it's just that they are not fully exercising their vocation in that place. They've allowed their job or ministry to tell them who they are rather than simply being who they are in their work.

In a spiritual sense, God rarely calls you to a particular ministry; that's the church's call. God calls you to a vocation, and then it's up to the community to discern with you the best place for you to exercise that call, given the community's needs and your particular gifts and talents.

We should never confuse the world's call—or even the church's call—with the Spirit's call. If that were the case, then apparently God never called a woman to leadership in most of our churches until about fifty years ago. In my own denomination, God must have had something against Blacks, making sure that we wouldn't be priests or bishops for much of our history in America. And God must be against those oriented to the same gender or diverse gender identities, having never called them to any ministry in the church, right? If it were God calling all the shots, then God obviously favors white straight males to pastor most of our largest parishes—and makes sure that they are paid better!

Properly speaking, then, God never called me to be an actor, a corporate financial representative, a college chaplain, parish pastor, diocesan staff person, cathedral canon, nor bishop. No, the business world and the various religious communities I was in called me to those positions—and I agreed with them. In each of these positions, I managed to find and proclaim good news, because that is what I do.

T HE IMPORTANT QUESTIONS to keep asking yourself are, "How can I be *here*, *now*? Am I being true to my call in this place? If not, when do I show up?" You cannot successfully transition from one stage to another unless you can affirmatively answer those questions of where you are *now*.

If *vocation* is God's call, and a particular *ministry* is the world's call, then *role* must surely be your call. You choose the role you play in any

The Spirit may be calling you to another stage in your life.

setting or situation. If Shakespeare is right, then everyone is granted several roles in the seven acts of the Grand Play of their life.

One role I've consistently played since I was a young child is that of peacemaker. This was an important role for me in my family of origin. I have been rewarded well, both emotionally and financially, for playing that role. It has helped me in my career as well as in my relationships. But playing the peacemaker role has also come at a cost—especially in those times when I've *overplayed* it. Some situations need to have real differences exposed, and sometimes heatedly worked out, in order to get to more liberating and lifegiving outcomes on the other side of the rupture. We are a more just and equitable society because some important conflicts have been acknowledged and painfully worked through rather than papered over. Of course, not every conflict can ever be successfully resolved, nor every problem solved, but incessant calls for "peace" without going through the needed conflict will result in nothing but making peace with injustice.

Unlike vocation, our roles are not a deep call of the Spirit. It's a mistake to confuse the role we play with who we essentially and indelibly are as a person. We assume our roles—sometimes out of necessity at the time, but rarely on a conscious level—because of the rewards we receive for playing the part. There is nothing wrong, of course, with playing a role, but if we keep playing the same role in every situation and ministry setting, then that gets boring and old—and not just for us!

Yes, I am a peacemaker, but I'm also—or I could be—many other things, depending on the situation. Maturity comes when a person is able to "see" themselves as more than the dominant role they've been playing for most of their life. Popular roles that many of us reflexively play are Parent, Judge, Questioner, Contrarian, Smartest Person in the Room, Compliant Daughter, Dutiful Son, Wallflower, Life of the Party, the One Who Shall Speak, the One Who Never Speaks, Clown, or Saint.

What is your dominant role in life? What is your go-to persona, and how have you been rewarded for it? Have you ever overplayed that role, becoming trapped into playing a part that is not always helpful or lifegiving to you?

The Spirit may be calling you to another stage in your life. That new stage will no doubt require you to grow into playing new roles that may be challenging for you. You may think that the new role is "not really me"—but just know that roles do not come from a deep place. They are what you learned to play as a response to some external situation that moved you to see yourself in that way. In the spiritual journey, there are always other possibilities that you may never have dreamed of as a role for you to play. God is not only the God of the present moment, but the God of a future that is waiting for you to walk into.

T HE IMPORTANT THING is to begin the journey. A grace-filled transition into a future that God sees for you will necessitate taking on some spiritual discipline that will allow you to be open to new possibilities. In this journey, you will not *think* your way into your next job or ministry; you will *pray* your way into it. This means taking on a contemplative spiritual discipline that will facilitate your being able to discern what that future could be.

Centering prayer is the critical practice that has enabled me to wade my way into exercising my vocation, living with integrity in every ministry setting, and learning not to get stuck in playing one role in every job. It has saved my life. I've been fortunate in my life to be endowed with many gifts and talents, but it took me several years of ordained ministry to come to the realization that my own power, skills, and creativity could only carry me for a while. There are only so many tricks in our bag, and that bag will eventually empty out. And, after a while, everybody knows our tricks anyway!

In contemplation, though, we descend daily into the well of infinite possibility. It is only in contemplative practice that we shut down our finite thinking, invite God's presence and action in our lives, and open ourselves to the Spirit's guidance. Contemplative prayer is the prayer of Jesus, who, on the night he transitioned from his earthly journey to life in its eternity, prayed to the Father, "Not my will, but Thy will be done" (Matthew 26:39). Opening ourselves up to the leading of the Holy Spirit is the only way to transition into the fullness of God's vision for our lives.

As I write this, I am in the process of yet another transition: I'll be retiring after sixteen wonderful years as bishop of the Diocese of Maryland in the spring of 2024. When I announced the timetable for my retirement, I had no plans for doing anything else, other than reading, traveling, sailing, and trying to hit a little white ball with a stick into a slightly larger hole hundreds of yards away. That was my plan.

God, of course (and my spouse, Sonya) laughed—both knowing me too well! Since announcing my transition, I've accepted the invitation of the Chautauqua Institution to become the Senior Pastor of that wonderful ecumenical and increasingly interfaith community in western New York. Chautauqua's summer program brings together prominent thought leaders and artists to explore the intersection of science, religion, the humanities, and the arts to explore the great questions of our times. We have vacationed and spoken there several times, and we look forward to making it our summer home.

So, once again, I prepare to exit one stage and enter another. My new ministry as a pastor brings me back full circle from my first ministry as a parish pastor over forty years ago. It will require me to dust off some old skills, learn new ones, and take on some roles that will be completely new to me. It will be an adventure, but so it always is on the journey. It really is true that we will play many parts on the stages of life. But, through it all, I keep in mind these other timeless words written by Shakespeare in *Hamlet*: "To thine own self be true."[4]

Be true to your calling, and may God bless you in all your moves and transitions in this earthly sojourn.   •

Santiago

The road seen, then not seen, the hillside hiding
then revealing the way you should take, the road
dropping away from you as if leaving you to walk
on thin air, then catching you, holding you up,
when you thought you would fall, and the way
forward always in the end the way that you followed,
the way that carried you into your future, that brought
you to this place, no matter that it sometimes took
your promise from you, no matter that it had to break
your heart along the way: the sense of having walked
from far inside yourself out into the revelation,
to have risked yourself for something that seemed
to stand both inside you and far beyond you,
that called you back in the end to the only road
you could follow, walking as you did, in your rags
of love and speaking in the voice that by night
became a prayer for safe arrival, so that one day
you realized that what you wanted had already
happened, and long ago and in the dwelling place
in which you had lived in before you began,

and that every step along the way, you had carried
the heart and the mind and the promise
that first set you off and then drew you on
and that, you were more marvelous in your
simple wish to find a way than the gilded roofs
of any destination you could reach:
as if, all along, you had thought the end point
might be a city with golden domes, and cheering
crowds, and turning the corner at what you thought
was the end of the road, you found just a simple
reflection, and a clear revelation beneath the face
looking back and beneath it another invitation,
all in one glimpse: like a person or a place
you had sought forever, like a broad field of freedom
that beckoned you beyond; like another life,
and the road still stretching on.

—David Whyte[1]

A Gentle Hum
of Spirit

By Sheryl Fullerton

W HEN I WAS a young college student, away from home for the first time and very much out of my depth, I lost my religion. I had grown up in Salt Lake City, the daughter of two apostate Mormons, but had connected deeply with the tradition during my childhood and adolescence, despite my parents' indifference (and occasional rancor). I loved the feeling of being part of my neighborhood's tight-knit congregation: singing in the choir, giving short talks in Sunday School, bearing witness to its truth in our main Sunday service, enjoying the midweek youth activities, participating in wholesome intramural sports, and teaching a class of three-year-olds their first lessons about God and Jesus. I believed devoutly, behaved impeccably, and belonged enthusiastically.

When I settled into that first semester at college, however, I failed to connect to those same kinds of activities in my new congregation. I was not known, not especially welcomed as yet another girl in a crowd of newcomers, and had no idea how to re-establish myself as part of the community. I missed that intense sense of belonging I had experienced at home. I was also more or less freaked out at living on my own for the first time, among strangers, most of whom were not Mormon, and preoccupied with adjusting to stiffer academic requirements.

I quit going to church all fall and winter, scrabbling to find footholds and friendships and figure out who I was now that I seemed no longer to be a "good Mormon girl." But in the spring, when I felt like I was on firmer ground, my conscience began to nag at me. I felt I needed to return to faith, but a conversation with the local bishop (the title Mormons use for the lay leader of a congregation) led nowhere. Maybe he was busy, weary of high-drama freshmen, but he didn't seem to register me as a person with heartfelt spiritual questions and needs. I was disappointed and gave up again until I went home for the summer. I was changing schools and was going to be living at home, so I decided to go back to the congregation that I'd always found such a haven.

But it wasn't the same. I was no longer a sweet teenager but a more skeptical college student who had gone away and was looking for reasons to come back. There wasn't much to bind me into the fold. The midweek group for young singles was boring and sparsely attended. The Sunday services seemed strangely narrow and dry, repetitions of rituals and propositions that I no longer quite believed. After a couple of months of trying, I drifted off again. Not long after, probably in part because it was 1969 and a time of social upheaval that the Mormon church furiously resisted and condemned, I rejected religion completely. I found new non-Mormon friends, took up smoking and drinking beer, hung around with philosophy and art majors, and told myself I was better off without any of it. If I felt any grief or sense of loss, I buried it or denied it, sure I had jettisoned some useless baggage.

I WOULDN'T HAVE CALLED this movement—this process of change from a settled religious identity to none at all—a transition, but it was one. I thought I was simply growing up and ending a naïve chapter in my life, with no other outcome in mind than abandonment. In a sense, I didn't even know what I was leaving because I had mistaken the container—the Mormon church—for the contents: the

Gospel and God and Jesus Christ. It was the only container I knew. When I rejected it, I didn't consider the possibility of other Christian options, unaware that I was losing something vital and essential it would take me years to recover.

For the next few years, I operated under the illusion that I didn't need any kind of religion. Then, a crisis at thirty sent me into therapy and a recognition that I wanted something more I couldn't quite name, like an itch I didn't know how to scratch. With the help of my therapist (a former Southern Baptist), I realized that what I lacked was an inner life, a life of spirit and meaning beyond the material. As a refugee from Christianity herself and a bold and curious seeker, she started me on a long season of wandering in the New Age and alternative world of do-it-yourself spirituality—Gaia worship, Native American spirituality, Wicca, Buddhism. I visited them all, but I could never quite attach to any of them. They didn't feel real to me. Despite outward appearances of participation, I felt like I was performing hollow approximations of another culture's spirituality.

About the time I turned fifty, weary of searching that had led nowhere but still full of yearning, I began another transition. As I left a Buddhist meditation session one Saturday morning, I thought, clearly, as though a voice were speaking out loud, "I'll never belong here. This is not my tradition. What is?" I now believe God was patiently waiting, like the prodigal son's father, for me to have this realization. But I wondered what could come next. I didn't know anything but Mormonism—and I wasn't going back there under any circumstances. Should I look to other forms of Christianity?

In an irony that I can only think of as providential, at about this time I was offered a job as a senior editor in religion and spirituality at a San Francisco publisher. I had some background in editing academic religious studies texts from a previous position and was intrigued by the kinds of books this publisher was handling. Somehow, I must have known that it was a calling more than just a job. I plunged in, full of questions: some theological, some ecclesiastical, many personal. I began to read: Stanley Hauerwas, Marcus Borg, C. S. Lewis, Henri Nouwen, Kathleen Norris, Thomas Merton, and many more, including the manuscripts that were now mine to shepherd to publication. It was an odd and rather random assortment of writers, but I had no one to guide me. I found I was ravening for insight and information so that I could assemble a vision of what it might mean for me to be Christian.

In any transition, there is a sense of grief, loss, and even anger at what is being left behind. In my twenties, when I abandoned Mormonism, I never acknowledged such feelings and told myself I was glad to be rid of it. But when I started investigating Christianity and looking for a church home, I was often filled with tremendous sadness. I cried when I sang hymns, even those I didn't know, or when we said the Lord's Prayer. I missed the familiarity of my original faith, even though I knew there was nothing there for me. For the first time, I truly felt the loss of what had held enormous meaning for me in my youth, even as I felt touched that God was mysteriously continuing to nudge my halting steps toward a new spiritual home.

In these explorations, I had to learn who Jesus was, beyond the picture in my childhood church of a blue-eyed, mild-mannered man gazing up to heaven. What did traditional Christians believe? Who was God to them? I became aware of the fractious and at times violent history of Christianity but also of saints and martyrs; creeds and schisms; social justice movements, pacifism, and liberation theology; and the different denominations and what they believed. Underlying it all was a gentle hum of spirit, leading me on, gripping me at times with intimations of what faith could be, and urging me to keep looking.

One day, a coworker mentioned how much she liked her Episcopal church in Berkeley. It was near where I was living, and I knew Episcopalians were among the more progressive and inclusive denominations, not just socially but also theologically. My growing sense of God was not the human-created patriarchal being I had encountered in Mormonism—or in many other Christian churches. I yearned to connect to a loving, generative God and to the deepest part of me—my True Self—and wanted a community that would help me do that.

In any transition, there is a sense of grief, loss, and even anger at what is being left behind.

THIS TRANSITION BACK into faith in that Berkeley church community was intentional, much more so than my departure into the spiritual wilderness in my twenties. I'm certain it was also God-inspired. As Isaiah 43:19 declares: "Behold, I am doing a new thing; now it springs forth, do you not perceive it? I will make a way in the wilderness and rivers in the desert." I had no idea where my journey would lead, but I was certain that it was mine to take, and that God would "make a way."

I had to learn many new things—liturgy, rituals, practices, traditions, hymns, theology, customs—all of which were entirely foreign to me. A Lenten catechumen class helped, but I still struggled with this new identity, an identity none of my secular friends shared and didn't quite understand. Yet I knew in my heart it was all worth it and trusted that, as eclectic Bay Areans, my friends would accept this new me. I persisted, gradually mastering the outward trappings of this new church while my inner convictions about the gracious invitation God was offering me grew and deepened. Conversations during this tender time, with authors I was editing as well as talented and faithful colleagues and clergy, also buoyed me, encouraged me, taught me, and confirmed me in my nascent faith.

I was baptized an Episcopalian on a cold March night, on Holy Saturday, along with my friend Sandy and two little red-headed girls, surrounded by the congregation I was coming to love and filled with the joy of spirit and candlelight and a historic liturgy. It was not an end point but a beginning. I knew I still had (and have) much to learn and to experience. As I wrote in my journal at that time, "God will lead me if I keep showing up. This isn't a club I'm joining, nor do I need to worry about anything. I just have to be present and let the experiences school me in being a Christian in community, in this particular community." Baptism wasn't an ending point. It was, in fact, preparation for the inevitable transitions to come, both in faith and in my life. •

The Disciples' Gospel:

The Transition from Believer to Disciple

By James P. Danaher

"On that day you will know that I am in my Father, and you in me, and I in you. They who have my commandments and keep them are those who love me, and those who love me will be loved by my Father, and I will love them and reveal myself to them." Judas (not Iscariot) said to him, "Lord, how is it that you will reveal yourself to us and not to the world?" Jesus answered him, "Those who love me will keep my word, and my Father will love them, and we will come to them and make our home with them. Whoever does not love me does not keep my words, and the word that you hear is not mine but is from the Father who sent me." (John 14:20-24)

Jesus' words to his disciples are instructions on how to bring his kingdom to earth. Keeping Jesus' words, however, is not something that we can do, but something that God must do through us as we yield our lives over to God. Jesus' life was yielded to the Father, and he is trying to teach his disciples how to yield their lives over to the Father as well. The way we yield our lives to the Father is through repentance (*metanoia*) or changing our minds about who we are.

We are all God's beloved daughters and sons. That is who we were made to be before the world got a hold of us and began making us into its likeness. In childhood, however, we were all wounded by the sin of the world, and we responded to those wounds the way the world taught us to respond. Those sins, and our worldly responses to them, went a long way in creating the person that we would eventually become in the world. That person that we and the world have created to be in the world can never see the beauty and goodness of Jesus' commandments to his disciples. That is because, from the level of consciousness that the world has given us, we see ourselves as isolated subjects surrounded by a world of threatening objects that we need to control and manipulate. From that level of consciousness, the words of Jesus make no sense, so we create doctrines and theologies that give us ways around Jesus' words.

Are we who Jesus says we are

There is, however, that deeper level of consciousness of who we were in God before the world got a hold of us and began making us into its likeness. This is the level of consciousness to which Jesus calls his disciples. This is the level of consciousness that we were "born from above" (John 3:3) to be, rather than the person the world has made us to be. Of course, to get to that deeper level of consciousness of who we were in God before the world got a hold of us and began making us into its likeness, we need to disidentify with the false self that we and the world have created to be in the world. This is the deep repentance to which Jesus calls his disciples. It is not a repentance or being sorrowful over a particular sin, but a repentance or changing our minds about who we ultimately are.

Are we who Jesus says we are or who the world says we are? If we identify with who the world says we are, we can believe that Jesus died for our sins, but we can never be his disciples, since disciples are those who take Jesus' words seriously and make his words their own. Making Jesus' words our own is not something that can be done from the level of consciousness that connects us to the world. From that level of consciousness, it seems crazy to love even our enemies (Matthew 5:44) and give to all who ask (Luke 6:30 and Matthew 5:42). From the perspective of the false self that we have created to be in the world, it makes no sense to refuse to respond to violence with violence (Matthew 5:39) or to love our neighbor in the same way that we love ourselves (Mark 12:31, Matthew 22:39, and Luke 10:27). Only the stillness of prayer can get us to that place where we can see how beautiful and good it is to forgive everyone (Matthew 6:15) and judge no one (Matthew 7:1–2). Contemplative prayer is what gets us to the place in God where we can see the beauty and goodness of Jesus' words and want those words to take root within us.

Wanting the hard words of Jesus to become our own is the narrow gate and hard road (Matthew 7:14) to which Jesus calls his disciples. Popular religion offers ways around that hard road by claiming that the right beliefs about Jesus' death and resurrection are sufficient to have our sins forgiven, and God's forgiveness of our sins is as far as most people want to go with Jesus. But Jesus never tells us what we

or who the world says we are?

must believe to have our sins forgiven. What he does tell his disciples is how they should be to bring his kingdom to earth. Jesus' words to his disciples are kingdom words, which are at odds with the world and who we are in the world.

From the level of consciousness that connects us to the world, we can believe that we are the objects of God's forgiveness, but Jesus' words to his disciples are about his disciples becoming the agents of God's forgiveness: "If you do not forgive others, neither will your Father forgive your trespasses" (Matthew 6:15). These words of Jesus to his disciples are not about how to receive God's forgiveness but about how to become God's forgiveness. Believers imagine that they are only guilty of the sins they have done and need to get forgiven, but Jesus tells his disciples that their sin, or what keeps them from the fullness of life in God, is also about the forgiveness, mercy, and love that they lack.

To see sin on this deeper level requires that we identify with who we are in God rather than who we are in the world, and that deeper identity requires a deeper level of prayer. The way we come to identify with who we are in God, rather than who we are in the world, is through the silence and stillness of prayer. If we practice this prayer enough that eventually we come to identify with who we are in God rather than who we are in the world, we begin to see the beauty and goodness of Jesus' words. Furthermore, if we continue to practice this prayer or level of consciousness that connects us to God rather than the world, we eventually find that more and more of our life is being lived out of this deeper level of consciousness that connects us to God rather than the world.

Jesus' words to his disciples are always about how to have that deeper interior life that Jesus had with his Father and our Father. Jesus is always calling his disciples to that deeper life of seeing themselves *in* God and God *in* them. This is who we were in God before the world got a hold of us and began making us into its likeness. It is why Jesus tells his disciples that they must become as little children (Matthew 18:3) or who they were in God before the world got a hold of them—and us—and began making us into its likeness.

THE SPIRITUAL JOURNEY to which Jesus calls his disciples is a matter of Jesus' words coming to life within us. Those words, however, cannot come to life within the person we have created to be in the world. The spiritual journey is about the progressive death of the false self so that our true self, or who we are in God, might come forth. Our only righteousness lies in who we are in God, and to try and make the false self that we have created to be in the world appear righteous is what Jesus called hypocrisy. The false self is always a pretense and an attempt to create an identity in other people's minds about who we are. The false self cannot be fixed or saved but must die if we are to find our true self in God. This is the spiritual journey—the Pilgrim's Progress—to which Jesus' disciples are called.

Believers trust their beliefs to save them because the words of Jesus make no sense from the perspective the world has given us. Disciples, however, no longer identify with the world and who they are in the world. Disciples identify with who they are in God and who God is in them. This is the level of consciousness that allows Jesus'

The end of the spiritual journey is to become disciples who realize that God is enough.

words to begin to take root within us, but we are never at the end of Jesus' words, and there are always deeper remnants of the false self that must die if we are to come more fully into our life in God.

Of course, we almost all begin as believers. It is not that the believers' gospel is a false gospel—it is just an elementary gospel. The spiritual life to which Jesus calls us is a matter of asking how much of Jesus' words we are willing to make our own and how much we are willing to allow the false self to die so we might come into that fullness of life in God.

Believers want God, but they want the world as well. The end of the spiritual journey is to become disciples who realize that God is enough and seek no happiness apart from God. When God is enough, the beauty and goodness of Jesus' words begin to take root within us, and we find those words beginning to direct our lives. This is the deeper life to which Jesus calls his disciples. It requires a repentance or changing our minds about who we really are. When Jesus addresses his disciples, he is addressing who they are in God rather than who they are in the world. When he addresses the religious people of his day, who saw themselves as righteous because of their religious beliefs, he calls them hypocrites (Matthew 23:13–15) for identifying with the false self or who they were created to be in the world rather than who they were in God.

Of course, the popular forms of Christianity have always presented a Jesus who is attractive to the level of consciousness that connects us to the world. Perhaps this is necessary since few of us are ready to become disciples until we can see the lie of the false self, and the only way we come to see that lie is by spending time alone with God and Jesus' words, which reveal our deeper life in God. The only way we come to realize that we have a deeper life in God is that we come to see the beauty and goodness of Jesus' words, which appear to be neither beautiful nor good from the perspective the world has given us. From the level of consciousness that connects us to the world, why would we wish to love our enemy (Matthew 5:44), to give to all who ask (Matthew 5:42), or refuse to respond to violence with violence (Matthew 5:39)? That is not how the world has taught us to be.

The beauty and goodness of Jesus' words only resonate with who we are in God rather than who we are in the world. This is the deeper life of the disciple, who lives in an almost constant state of repentance because their time alone with God has brought them to see both the beauty and goodness of Jesus' words and how their life in the world is at odds with those words. •

The Color of Thought

By Sophfronia Scott

T HE SUMMER BEFORE my senior year in high school, I attended a program at the Ohio State University called the Martin W. Essex School for the Gifted. The participants were the top students in the state. It was a miraculous time because so many of us had been made to feel bad about ourselves because we got good grades and liked to read. That week, we learned there was nothing wrong with us, and we reveled in our shared interests.

We were a diverse group. I had grown up with such diversity in Lorain, Ohio, a proverbial melting pot because so many people of varied cultural backgrounds lived there to work in the factories. My own father worked in the steel mill.

I was excited to make new friends, but there was one student I didn't want to befriend—in fact, I tried to avoid him. Picture a cross between Brad Pitt and Tom Cruise: blond and carefree with a high-wattage smile. He came from a wealthy family. I felt he was someone who would automatically look down on me—guys like him were not nice to girls like me.

One day, we ended up in a room alone. There had been two other students present, and I had focused my attention on them. One of them was blind and when he had to go to the bathroom, my other friend escorted him because he was unfamiliar with the building. That left me with Mr. Hollywood Smile.

We began to talk. His name was Kurt, and we began a conversation that not only continued after my friends returned, but went on to become a correspondence after the program was over. I can't tell you everything we learned about each other, but I left that room with a pain I still think about today: the realization that I almost didn't make this connection with Kurt because I had been prejudiced against him. I had made and acted on assumptions that were wrong, the main one being that he would be prejudiced against me.

In light of our present moment, when names such as Brionna Taylor, George Floyd, and Ahmaud Arbery remain on our hearts and the news still features stunning images of inequality, what I'm about to put forth may seem naïve or even pollyannish. However, as a writer, I tend to move toward what I feel isn't said enough or isn't being heard—and it's the moving that's important, however imperfect.

THE HIDDEN WHOLENESS

THE MONK THOMAS MERTON (1915–1968) began his 1962 prose poem "Hagia Sophia" with:

> There is in all things an invisible fecundity, a dimmed light, a meek namelessness, a hidden wholeness. . . . There is in all things an inexhaustible sweetness and purity, a silence that is a fount of action and joy.[1]

Merton connected this "mysterious unity" with wisdom, but I connect this "hidden wholeness" with his famous epiphany at Fourth and Walnut, which I believe flows with the same gentleness, sweetness, and humility of which he writes in "Hagia Sophia."

> I was suddenly overwhelmed with the realization that I loved all those people, that they were mine and I theirs, that we could

not be alien to one another even though we were total strangers. It was like waking from a dream of separateness, of spurious self-isolation in a special world, the world of renunciation and supposed holiness.... Now I realize what we all are. And if only everybody could realize this! But it cannot be explained. There is no way of telling people that they are all walking around shining like the sun.[2]

Notice he doesn't define a specific race. He doesn't say white people or black people or brown people. "They are *all* walking around shining like the sun." *We* are all walking around shining like the sun. *We* as human beings, each one of us, is a tremendous miracle, separate as individuals and yet deeply connected. I was once asked in an interview what stance Merton would take on this question: "All lives matter, Black Lives Matter, or in some way both?" I replied that I felt Merton would say all lives matter, but we don't act like it. If we did, we wouldn't have to insist that Black lives matter. If we did, we would sense how wounded we are when we don't rise and declare our brothers and sisters—not some undefined "other"—are threatened.

WHY IS THE WHOLENESS HIDDEN?

THIS DEBATE OF all lives matter versus Black lives matter exists because our wholeness is hidden. It is hidden because of the way we see the world. Whenever I hear someone want to insist that all lives matter, I want to ask, "Why do you feel this must be expressed?" because at the heart of this question, it sounds like someone feels they are being left out, devalued, or ignored. I don't understand—and I want to understand. We all must try to understand each other.

This understanding puts us on the path to grasping the wholeness, of understanding our unity, and it seems to me we can't grasp that. We need our categorizations—and we are blinded when we only see our differences.

Josephine Baker, the famous entertainer who rocketed to fame and fortune and became the toast of Paris in the 1920s, adopted twelve children from all over the world, places like Japan, Finland, Algeria, and Colombia. She called them her "rainbow tribe" and said they "were all adopted to come down here to prove that human beings could live together. They might have different pigmentations and come from different continents, but that has nothing to do with the human being."[3]

Two of these children, now adults, were interviewed and asked, "What would you say your mother's legacy is?"

Their reply: "Her ideal of universal brotherhood; it was very important for her."[4]

But here's an archived interview with Baker herself showing how bewildering that concept was. The reporter had asked Baker if she thought she would "serve your race" far better if she had remained in the US instead of going back to Europe.

Baker: "My race?"
Reporter: "The Negro race."
Baker: "Ah ha. You see, I think a little differently. For me, there is only one race: the human race."
Reporter: "How long are you going to stay?"
Baker: "You want me to stay, don't you?"
Reporter: "I'd like you to stay. I think you could help the Negro movement in the United States."
Baker: "Oh, don't say that."
Reporter: "Why not?"
Baker: "Because it's not a Negro movement. It's an American movement."[5]

The reporter doesn't get it. He can't grasp Baker's deep sense of unity.

Now, fast forward to November 2014.

Here's the author Toni Morrison, in an interview with Stephen Colbert:

Colbert: "You've said you don't necessarily like to be pigeonholed as an African American writer. What would you like me to pigeonhole you as? I have to categorize everybody. Do you wanna be, you know, pigeonholed as a Korean pop star? How should I see you as a category? If you don't want to be an African American writer, how should I think of you?"

Often, "doing something" leads
to grand gestures that overlook
the small changes we could be
making in our individual lives.

Morrison: "As an American writer. There is no such thing as race—none. There's just a human race, scientifically, anthropologically. Racism is a construct, a social construct, and it has benefits. Money can be made off of it and people who don't like themselves can feel better because of it. It can describe certain kinds of behavior that are wrong or misleading, so it has a social function. But race can only be defined as a human being."[6]

Colbert changed the subject, going on to make a joke. Granted, he only had seven minutes, and these important words require so much more time—I'd say generations—to process. He moved on. But we all move on from thinking about this because this big concept calls us to look at all aspects of our lives, from small, seemingly insignificant moments to the huge and bewildering tragedies and the recognition that another human being—a brother, a sister—has been treated as "less than" and we must do something about it.

However, we tend to think that "doing something" is an all-or-nothing, zero-sum game in which someone has to lose something in order for progress to happen. If we focus on Black Lives Matter, somebody thinks their life matters less. If we have affirmative action, someone thinks a position is being taken from them to be given to someone else. This heightens tensions and doesn't address the fact that—and here's where unity is hard and messy—the sense of fear, loss, and pain is valid. If we don't acknowledge that, the space tightens—it's harder to make space for all voices because all voices aren't heard or respected, even if they don't agree. We deny each other's humanity when we insist that there is an accounting, and someone must gain, and someone must lose. In the end, we all lose because we've failed to see how connected we are.

Often, "doing something" leads to grand gestures that overlook the small changes we could be making in our individual lives—changes in both our behaviors and our thinking that could lead to real change. An entrepreneur contacted me recently to ask my opinion of a project that involved selling rings. He promoted wearing one of these rings as "a concrete action toward creating a more just and equitable world" because some of the funds raised would go to causes "doing meaningful social justice work."

He told me the project came about because he's a member of a referral group, and one day they looked around the room and realized there were no people of color in the room. They decided to "do something" and that led to the ring.

"It's a referral group?" I asked. "People in the room invite people they know, like, and trust, right?"

"Right."

"If people of color are not in the room, that means they don't know anyone they would invite."

"Yes, I guess that's true."

"What are your group members doing, as individuals, to change who is in their lives so the people in the room can change?"

He couldn't answer that question. We had a vague discussion about the ages of the people in the room and how it's harder to make that kind of change. I told him I understood, but while the ring project is a valid one, I urged him to encourage the group to do the harder work.

As much as racism is about addressing systemic changes, it is also about the personal conversions that must take place in individual hearts.

THE AUTHOR BRYAN Massingale, in his lecture "Engaging Racism: Thomas Merton, the Church, and the Ongoing Quest for Justice," said, "Racism is not a matter of intellect. Racism grips us in the guts. It's a matter that speaks deeply to who we are or who we think we are."[7]

Racism is indeed deeply personal. Wrestling with it can only be done, not by asking someone else to educate us or by reading a book, although those may be starting points, but by asking ourselves the hard questions. This is because, as much as racism is about addressing systemic changes, it is also about the personal conversions that must take place in individual hearts. Merton knew this when he wrote in "Letters to a White Liberal," "We are forced to admit that the Civil Rights legislation is not the end of the battle but only *the beginning of a new and more critical phase in the conflict.*"[8]

This big piece of legislation had been passed, but it didn't mean that people had changed.

How does the individual move toward such conversion? We will each travel our own way but, however we walk, the journey will take us toward honing hearts of compassion. Massingale points out that Merton's insights are grounded in a profound spiritual experience: His Fourth and Walnut epiphany, which moved Merton to live not in the head, but from the heart—and, I would add, from the soul—came from a compassion born of his deep contemplation.

People have asked how Merton could be relevant to any of the social issues he addressed because he wasn't really in the world—he was a cloistered monk, after all. But the work he did on himself made him relevant. He understood the power of nonviolence because he recognized where, in his own life, he wasn't practicing it. For example, he recognized he wasn't practicing nonviolence when he was always in a defensive stance, disagreeing with his superiors. He knew the powerful combination of prayer and study it required. He shared with novices the preparation that the protestors who worked with Dr. Martin Luther King Jr. had to follow, including reading Scripture.

Even if you can't commit to this type of study, you can challenge yourself to understand your own thoughts and ideas, especially if you find yourself following the herd. In high school, I had to ask myself,

"Why was I so prejudiced against Kurt? And am I treating anyone else like this in my life?"

Merton's hope for humanity, for all of us, was working toward embracing our unity—the unity we share with each other and our creator. Working on ourselves may seem like a small thing, like we are all mere drops in the ocean. But we are an ocean. We must grasp that because, as Bryan Massingale said, "People will not do the hard, serious, difficult work that authentically confronting racism demands unless they are grounded in something that is greater and deeper than themselves. We need then a counternarrative that grounds another identity that is different than the one offered by US society with its polarizations."[9]

I say this counternarrative is the story of our unity.   •

Transition

By Paula D'Arcy

Our lives forever shift in new directions,
pulling us like the moon pulls the tides.

FOR OVER TWO decades, David Whyte's poetry has opened me to the great journey it is to live in this world. Some transitions move slowly, requiring years of patience, waiting for a moment of readiness. It is not unlike the nine months when a woman gestates a seed prior to the minute of birth. All seeds require care. In Italian, the words *Dare alla Luce* (to give birth) literally mean "to bring to the light." Every transition shares this same potential. We're always learning what life can be.

An unexpected phone call in 1976 became a moment of birth for me. A dear friend was visiting, and my nine-month-old daughter Beth was sitting happily on her lap as Marion read to her. I was twenty-eight years old and still finding my way after surviving an accident set in motion by a drunk driver just a year before. My husband and twenty-two-month-old daughter Sarah were both killed, and I was left, three months pregnant, to grieve my lost dreams and face an unknown future.

Now a Connecticut court official was on the other end of the line, asking me, as required by law, how I wanted the driver who had caused this accident to be treated. Implied were the words *how harshly*. In that moment, I remembered what a Native American elder who gave talks in the town where I grew up said to us one night: "When you speak a word, the sound never stops."

The court official told me some details about the driver's life. I asked myself what I really knew about such a journey: nothing, if I was being truthful. I didn't know if he'd ever been loved, or any of the ways his own life had been broken. I kept thinking about the sound that never stops.

I heard my daughter's laughter from the next room while the official waited for me to respond. I was certain that Beth would not avoid the pain of growing up without a father; she would suffer that loss. But another realization came to me: That my response to the official was what Beth would inherit from me, her mother. She would inherit the sound of my word.

What I didn't know that day, but learned years later, was that what I prescribed for the driver I was also prescribing for myself. We are not separate; all life is intricately intertwined. When I asked for the driver to receive help in order to heal, I unknowingly opened that future for myself as well. And in thinking about words whose sound never stops, I felt for the first time a real responsibility in being here and choosing the power of my words and actions, a sense of life's deeper meaning. Years in the future, a teacher would say to me that *the great transition of our times, of all times, is to see what we don't yet see.*

"Struggling souls catch light from other souls," writes author Clarissa Pinkola Estes, and "what is needed . . . is an accumulation of acts, adding, adding to, adding more."[1] In 1975, I only longed for my old life, even though I knew I couldn't have it back. Everything else in my life was undiscovered. I was in between those two places and unable to see any potential that might lie ahead. Yet, somewhere in my childhood, I had caught light from that Native teacher, and decades later the sound of his words helped me make that transition.

Once, on a walking pilgrimage from Paris to the great Gothic cathedral in Chartres, France, I had a dream. I dreamed about the men who had first laid the stones for that cathedral eight hundred years

The great transition of our times, of all times, is to see what we don't yet see.

before, pulling them by rope from the quarry and then dragging them for miles to the building site. Just before waking, while still dreaming, I saw myself standing at the newly dug foundation of that cathedral. I heard my name, and when I turned around, the next stone was passed to me.

That stone became a symbol of great consequence for me. I was no longer watching life take place. As I stretched out my arms to receive it, I knew myself to be a participant in the great flow of life, connected to the past but, even more so, to the future. Life is forever in motion and so are we. Everything is in a continual process of becoming. Like the ocean rising and falling in response to the moon, we rise and fall.

Diarmuid O'Murchu speaks about our need to relate to life in a different way, to re-vision what it means to be human, because what it means to be fully human is what we still don't know. He writes, "Humanity today needs a new mindset . . . a capacity for deep seeing."[2]

Wanting things to remain the same had prevented me from seeing what was always present: the ability to "add, add to"; to make choices; to evolve as the universe is evolving; to take part in what Joanna Macy calls "the great turning."[3]

In time, I read the words of Thomas Merton (1915–1968): "I was not sure where I was going and I could not see what I would do when I got there . . . [yet] a track led me across the waters to a place I had never dreamed of."[4] I understood Merton's meaning. Reaching forward had put me face to face with ordinary moments that begged to be seen in their depth.

In the 1990s, I heard author Frederick Buechner (1926–2022) tell a story from his time teaching at Exeter Academy.[5] He described a late afternoon class where the young students were fidgeting and restless.

Then, on impulse, he snapped off the classroom lights. As soon as it went dark, the entire sky outside the classroom windows blazed with a fiery sunset. Buechner remembered that for twenty minutes, no one moved or spoke. Afterward, he said that watching the sunset that afternoon was more important than anything else that happened that year. They had moved from the lesson plan and theories about life to life itself. They moved from imagining life to touching it directly, and for that moment they were bound together.

While attending an online global prayer gathering for peace in 2022, I listened to an aid worker tell a story that reminded me of the timeless moment that happened in Buechner's classroom. She had witnessed something during the early days of the invasion of Ukraine, when the main square in Kiev had just been decimated. One Russian soldier found himself alone in the center of the square facing a crush of grief-stricken Ukrainians. The soldier was in his twenties and caught in a terrible place. The large group of Ukrainians continued to press forward until they formed a circle around him.

But then a Ukrainian woman stepped forward with great dignity, handed him a bowl of soup, and urged him to eat because he must be hungry. The young boy received her offering, gratefully tipped the bowl to his lips, and drank. When the bowl was emptied, a second woman stepped forward, held out her cell phone, and urged the soldier to call his mother because she must be worried sick, wondering if he was alive.

It's impossible to know what was rising up in those two Ukrainian women that day, or what transitions might have long preceded that circle in the square. But something of great beauty suddenly blossomed

What does it mean to take
responsibility for the world,
to see beneath the
surface of
things?

and was expressed. They stood knee deep in rubble that afternoon, the destruction of their city happening at the hands of an army to which this soldier belonged. The grief and pain in life usually seek a swift punishment, not an unreasonable act of love. *Acts, adding, adding to, adding more.* No one spoke as the bowl of soup was offered within that small circle and bound them together.

T HERE ARE DAYS, say the poets, when our lives could go one way or another. In the circle in Kiev, the "next stone" being handed to the first woman was the Russian soldier. The stone being offered to the soldier was a bowl of soup. Everything was carried by the one rising tide. And the silent questions echo: *What wants to be brought alive? How much are we willing to see? Can we go beyond our conditioning into something new?*

Transitions are not about resisting life but awakening within it: *Seeing the depth of the ordinary moment until a heartbroken woman facing a soldier reveals all that we might be.* Dare alla Luce. *Being present to life in a way that accounts for love.* Author Stephanie Saldana writes about moments when everything appears different than before, "as if I had been closing my eyes for an entire lifetime."[6]

What does it mean to take responsibility for the world, to see beneath the surface of things?

In July of 2020, I attended a six-day virtual choir festival at a time when no choirs were able to gather and sing because of the pandemic. We watched films and heard talks and one night closed with musician Ken Medema singing the lullaby, "All Through the Night." He told us that on the last iteration of the chorus, he would remain silent so that hundreds of us, muted in our homes and our countries, could softly sing the refrain ourselves: "all through the night."

He brought us in with the verse: "Sleep my child and peace attend thee," then stopped and waited. And at our desks, in our living rooms, sitting on the floor, wherever we were, we sang, "all through the night."

Again, after "while the moon her watch is keeping," he held up his hand for our silent chorus: "all through the night."

At first, I sang along. I turned off the lights in my room, sitting only with the blue-white glow from the computer: "all through the night," for two or three repetitions, watching people's mouths move, but hearing only silence. I sang until I could no longer sing, overtaken by the two hundred voices I couldn't hear, but then *did* begin to hear, somehow, across thousands of miles . . . although surely I was not hearing with my ears. It broke me. I imagined gulls soaring above the marshes and the sea.

The silence was strangely more impacting, more intimate, than if I were physically hearing choirs singing in full voice. In that simple refrain, I listened to my own life journey—every place I'd ever been, every disappointment that had been suffered, every betrayal, every transition that moved me to a new understanding of love and responsibility, every time I managed to say yes to life. Every moment, dark or light—the hard-won moments, the drunk driver's future, and the swell of seagulls overhead—all were stones lovingly placed into my hands with the choice of whether or not to receive them. With each bowl of soup, the world rises and falls, saying, "It's time to do more, to be better."

The awakening to love is long and labored: the love which holds the world, which holds the possibility of war and peace, which holds us as we repair what has been torn apart, which guides us to what time cannot touch. The love that is everywhere is in seed. "Love that illumines every broken thing it finds," writes Jan Richardson.[7] That shift moves us from thinking about "life in general" to an encounter with *this* moment, *this* sunset, *this* swelling tide, *this* word whose sound will never stop, *this* transition making way for the next, greater expression of love. *Adding to, adding more.* "We have to find a wiser way to live,"[8] writes author Jack Kornfield. I agree. This is our moment. •

RECOMMENDED READING

Let Your Heartbreak Be Your Guide:
Lessons in Engaged Contemplation

Adam Bucko
Orbis Books, October 2022

A Book Review by Paul Swanson

> *We awaken in Christ's body just as Christ awakens our bodies.*
> —St. Symeon the New Theologian[1]

EPISCOPAL PRIEST Fr. Adam Bucko's *Let Your Heartbreak Be Your Guide: Lessons in Engaged Contemplation* moves like a river. What I like about rivers is that they show up all at once. The flow of a river *is* the fullness and immediacy of their life. I used to think a river operated more mechanically, that upriver transported the blessed current moment from the past to the present, catching its breath before sending it forth to touch the future downriver. I was corrected by poet Jim Harrison, who writes that "moving water is forever in the present tense, a condition we rather achingly avoid."[2] True enough, but it was only when braving this condition via a full-body immersion into a shockingly swift and cold river that I was able to see the error in my mechanical thinking. All that a river can be is present in the totality of its flow. Moving water awakens me to the immediacy and fullness of life. It is in this sense that *Let Your Heartbreak Be Your Guide* reads like a river, awakening the way of engaged contemplation.

The awakening flow of *Let Your Heartbreak Be Your Guide* is needed in times like ours. The fog of suffering is thick on the skin, and the confusion of the pandemic is hard to shake. The cries of the poor are being exploited by the catcalls of politicians. Corporations are salting the earth and forcing forests into early retirement. Because of all this, there is a nostalgic longing by some for yesterdays that felt clear and principled. There is an ache in others for an unblemished and automated utopian future. We are handcuffed to distractions and in desperate need of a key to snap out of it. Fr. Bucko offers such a key in engaged contemplation, which is moving *with* the suffering in the achingly present, inhaling the fumes of fear and exhaling lovingkindness. We are called to abide in and swim in this flow of love "that helps us live by the way of listening and responding to God in our midst."[3]

Let Your Heartbreak Be Your Guide has a contagious momentum.[4] The flux of the book is found in three major sections: Listening to Life, Touch What Frightens Us, and Interrupting Silence. The three terracing sections move as one toward a ribboning waterfall. The stories and reflections cascade the reader toward a surrender of purpose: on being a contemplative in the world[5] where the page ends and the reader's life begins.

LISTENING TO LIFE

W HEN WE READ a religious or spiritual book, what motivates us to pick it up? Is it the acquisition of knowledge or perspective? Perhaps we are seeking personal or communal guidance? My motivation lies with each of those, but it begins with a trust that the author is able to articulate their own allurement toward Mystery.

Fr. Bucko moves through the pages of this incarnational book with honesty and wonder. He shares stories of his life to centralize the unfolding and graced perspective of a life seeking to live out of the presence of God: from his childhood in totalitarian Poland, serving LGBTQIA+ youth and homeless on the streets of New York City, discernment of priesthood, engaging with the elders who encouraged his quest, confronting death in exchange for a more vulnerable life, and facing the desert places with unscaled eyes to grow in compassionate action. These stories are the ripple effect of the rich mystical traditions that flow through the life of Fr. Adam Bucko.

TOUCHING WHAT FRIGHTENS US

IN OUR CACOPHONIC hours, Fr. Bucko instructs us to not "be afraid to have a heart and to risk breaking your heart. Feel into it all and know that every time you are touching the pain, you are touching the sacred wound of God."[6] The way of Jesus encourages us to bear witness, suffer with others, and be prayerful wounded healers. When we courageously move toward our fears with faith that the heart of Divine Mystery beats and breaks with our own, we can imagine that, in some mysterious way, transformation is possible.

In this section of the book, Fr. Bucko exemplifies this movement by drawing us into the pain of bearing the grief of a friend's murder and enduring crushing systemic power, refugee camps, and the ongoing global pandemic. Crises are experienced personally and collectively and can reshape our relationship to reality. Fr. Bucko challenges us to wake up to reality and reshape our relationships, to see our complicity and our ignorance in the suffering world, which is a resurrection in waiting. In reflection upon the pandemic, he writes that the "resurrection that we await isn't about returning to normal; it is about transformation. It is about change that you and I can commit to after this immense suffering."[7]

INTERRUPTING SILENCE

PEOPLE IN CONTEMPLATIVE circles are tempted to silently step out of the fray of a mutinous reality to protect false peace. Fr. Bucko calls us to a contemplation that resonates with the life of Jesus, to be engaged with the world *as it is*, "to let go of any illusions we harbor that the spiritual life is about anything other than learning to travel and struggle and love and depend on one another, together, no matter how messy it gets."[8] Living in the uncurated present moment is a fruit of contemplation, a desire to see each interruption as bumping into the generosity of God.

The invitation to this portion of *Let Your Heartbreak Be Your Guide* is vividly portrayed in the story of a young man living in homelessness and with the private diagnosis of HIV. He pays attention to the growing call on his life to be a public spokesperson and mentor for those also living with HIV/AIDS. The discernment and risk of that decision break forth into a freedom that enables him "to show up for others in a new way and with a new hope."[9] In humble acceptance, this young man's life preaches that these uninvited intrusions of life can somehow, in some way, become purposeful exchanges of Christ freely given and received, if only we have eyes to see. The circumstances may be different, but each reader will find themselves in this series of interruptions and opportunities. You will ask yourself: What might happen if I allow myself to be emptied of agendas to follow the whyless way of love?

The collected stories and practices in *Let Your Heartbreak Be Your Guide* will help you advance, build, and draw together a compelling vision of a life lived in, with, and for love. As you reach the end, your heart will be broken open and your feet will be dangling in the river of presence. Quoting Madeleine Delbrel (1904–1964), Fr. Bucko offers a refreshed way of understanding ourselves as contemplatives in the world "because we find that love is work enough for us, we don't take the time to categorize what we are doing as either 'contemplation' or 'action.'"[10] From this riverbank, Fr. Bucko offers guidance on immersing yourself into deeper waters with practices that can teach you to not shrink in the face of suffering, but kiss her cheek; to help you welcome sister death; and, most importantly, an embodied perspective that cultivates an ear to hear the Divine's voice in storm and stillness.

Let Your Heartbreak Be Your Guide: Lessons in Engaged Contemplation is as full and immediate as a river. It traces the confluence of prayer and justice in the present tense. It asks us to risk full-body immersion for the purpose of awakening in Christ's body just as Christ awakens in our bodies. Come on in. It is an indelible swim. •

NOTES

Introduction

1 Brian D. McLaren, *Do I Stay Christian? A Guide for the Doubters, the Disappointed, and the Disillusioned* (New York: St. Martin's, 2022), 57–58.

2 McLaren, *Do I Stay Christian*, 56–57.

3 McLaren, *Do I Stay Christian*, 57.

4 McLaren, *Do I Stay Christian*, 57.

5 Cedar Ridge Community Church.

Liminality and Certitude

1 Felicia Murrell, "Liminality and Certitude," © 2021, previously unpublished.

The Hero's Journey

1 Barry Lopez, *Crossing Open Ground* (New York: Charles Scribner's Sons, 1988), 69.

2 Mircea Eliade, *The Sacred and the Profane: The Nature of Religion* (New York: Harcourt, 1957).

3 Richard Rohr, *True Self/False Self* (Cincinnati: Franciscan Media, 2013), 5 CDs; 6 hours.

4 Dante Alighieri, *Paradiso* 33:145.

5 Joseph Campbell, *The Hero with a Thousand Faces* (Princeton: Bollingen, 1949), 30.

In Times of Turbulence, Fly Loose

1 Kamea Chayne and Bayo Akomolafe, "Bayo Akomolafe: Slowing Down and Surrendering Human Centrality," *Green Dreamer* podcast,

episode 317, https://greendreamer.com/podcast/dr-bayo-akomolafe-the-emergence-network.

2 Rami Shapiro and Matthew Fox, "Cosmic Wisdom and the Divine Feminine: Lost Insights for an Emerging World," Session III, *Convergence*, https://convergencecolab.org/p/cosmic-wisdom-and-the-divine-feminine.

3 Jean Houston, "Mything Links," *Facebook*, March 13, 2021, https://www.facebook.com/notes/10240701246866782/.

4 Thomas Berry, *The Dream of the Earth* (Berkeley: Counterpoint Press, 2015), 42.

5 Thomas Merton, *Thoughts in Solitude* (New York: Farrar, Straus and Giroux, 1958), 79.

6 Chayne and Akomolafe, "Bayo Akomolafe."

Standing in a Threshold

1 United States Catholic Conference, "Called and Gifted for the Third Millennium, 1995," *United States Conference of Catholic Bishops*, https://www.usccb.org/committees/laity-marriage-family-life-youth/called-and-gifted-third-millennium-1995.

2 Cathleen Falsani, "In New Book, Richard Rohr Says the 'Universal Christ' Changes Everything," *National Catholic Reporter*, April 1, 2019, https://www.ncronline.org/spirituality/new-book-richard-rohr-says-universal-christ-changes-everything.

3 Richard Rohr, *Falling Upward: A Spirituality for the Two Halves of Life* (San Francisco: Jossey-Bass, 2011), 89.

4 Rohr, *Falling Upward*, 114.

5 Center for Action and Contemplation, "Transforming Ourselves, Each Other, and the World," *CAC*, https://cac.org/about/what-we-do/.

6 Center for Action and Contemplation, "The Living School," *CAC*, https://cac.org/living-school/living-school-welcome/.

7 Center for Action and Contemplation, "Admissions," *CAC*, https://cac.org/living-school/admissions/.

The Transition of Founders

1 Rachel Muir, "How to Survive Nonprofit Founder's Syndrome," *Bloomerang*, https://bloomerang.co/blog/how-to-survive-nonprofit-founders-syndrome/.

2 Chuck DeGroat, *When Narcissism Comes to Church: Healing Your Community from Emotional and Spiritual Abuse* (Downers Grove, IL: InterVarsity Press, 2020), 59.

Transitions and the Roles We Play

1 William Shakespeare, *As You Like It*, Act II, sc. vii.

2 Frederick Buechner, *Wishful Thinking: A Theological ABC* (New York: Harper & Row, 1973), 95.

3 Parker Palmer, *Let Your Life Speak: Listening for the Voice of Vocation* (San Francisco: Jossey-Bass, 2000), 3.

4 William Shakespeare, *Hamlet*, Act I, sc. iii.

Santiago

1 *David Whyte: Essentials* (2020) and *Pilgrim* (2012). ©2012 David Whyte and Many Rivers Press. www.davidwhyte.com.

The Color of Thought

1 Thomas Merton, *In the Dark Before Dawn: New Selected Poems*, ed. Lynn R. Szabo (New York: New Directions, 2005), 65.

2 Thomas Merton, *Conjectures of a Guilty Bystander* (New York: Image Books, 2014), 153.

3 *CBS Sunday Morning*, "The Legacy of Josephine Baker," aired December 5, 2021 on CBS, https://www.cbsnews.com/news/the-legacy-of-josephine-baker/.

4 *CBS Sunday Morning*, "Legacy of Josephine Baker."

5 *CBS Sunday Morning*, "Legacy of Josephine Baker."

6 *The Colbert Report*, Season 11, "Toni Morrison," aired November 19, 2014 on Comedy Central, https://www.cc.com/video/9yc4ry/the-colbert-report-toni-morrison.

7 Bryan Massingale, "Engaging Racism: Thomas Merton, the Church, and the Ongoing Quest for Justice," *The Thomas Merton Center*, 4th Annual Thomas Merton Black History Month Lecture, February 22, 2010, http://www.merton.org/Research/AV/av.aspx?id=406.

8 Thomas Merton, *Seeds of Destruction* (New York: Farrar, Straus and Giroux, 1964), 4.

9 Massingale, "Engaging Racism."

Transition

1 Clarissa Pinkola Estes, "You Were Made for This," *Awakin*, https://www.awakin.org/v2/read/view.php?tid=548.

2 Diarmuid O'Murchu, *Beyond the Pandemic: Spiritual and Ecological Challenges* (Maryknoll, NY: Orbis, 2022), 153.

3 Joanna Macy, "The Great Turning," *Center for Ecoliteracy*, June 29, 2009, https://www.ecoliteracy.org/article/great-turning.

4 Thomas Merton, *The Seven Storey Mountain* (New York: Harcourt, Brace and Company, 1948), 132.

5 Frederick Buechner, "Sunset," *FrederickBuechner*, May 26, 2019, https://www.frederickbuechner.com/quote-of-the-day/2019/5/26/sunset.

6 Stephanie Saldana, *The Bread of Angels: A Journey to Love and Faith* (Toronto: Doubleday, 2010), 119.

7 Jan Richardson, *Circle of Grace: A Book of Blessings for the Seasons* (Orlando: Wanton Gospeller Press, 2015), 48.

8 Jack Kornfield, *The Wise Heart: A Guide to the Universal Teachings of Buddhist Psychology* (New York: Bantam, 2008), 8.

Recommended Reading

1 Adam Bucko, *Let Your Heartbreak Be Your Guide: Lessons in Engaged Contemplation* (New York: Orbis, 2022), 112.

2 Jim Harrison, *Off to the Side: A Memoir* (New York: Grove Press, 2002), 1.

3 Bucko, *Let Your Heartbreak*, 127.

4 I had the intuition that if I set this book down for too long it would drift downstream into the hands of another eager reader.

5 The "Afterword: On Being a Contemplative in the World" and "Appendix of Spiritual Practices" are the map and means for the embodiment of that presence in the world.

6 Bucko, *Let Your Heartbreak*, 132.

7 Bucko, *Let Your Heartbreak*, 73.

8 Bucko, *Let Your Heartbreak*, 91.

9 Bucko, *Let Your Heartbreak*, 110.

10 Bucko, *Let Your Heartbreak*, 126.

Coming Fall 2023!

Falling Upward, Vol. 11, No. 2

INSPIRED BY ONE OF Richard Rohr's most popular books, *Falling Upward: A Spirituality for the Two Halves of Life*, this issue of *Oneing* will feature contributors who are struggling with the challenges of the first half of life, those who are entering into the second half of life, and those who have experienced both and are ready to fully move on to the "further journey."

In *Falling Upward*, Rohr helps us to understand the tasks of the two halves of life and teaches us that those who have failed, or gone down, are the only ones who can really understand the meaning of "up." Those who have somehow fallen, and fallen well, are the only ones who can grow spiritually and not misuse "up." In the words of Richard Rohr's favorite English mystic, Julian of Norwich (1343–1416), "First the fall, and then the recovery from the fall, and both are the mercy of God."

We look forward to what promises to be an intriguing journey.

Both the limited-print edition of CAC's literary journal, *Oneing*, and the downloadable PDF version will be available for sale in the Fall of 2023 at https://store.cac.org/.